101 Easy Reading Games Grade 5

by Margaret Fetty

Published by
Frank Schaffer Publications®

Author: Margaret Fetty
Editors: Kim Bradford, Sara Bierling

Frank Schaffer Publications ®

Send all inquiries to:
Frank Schaffer Publications
8720 Orion Place
Columbus, Ohio 43240-2111

101 Easy Reading Games—grade 5
ISBN: 0-7682-3415-8

1 2 3 4 5 6 7 8 9 MAZ 11 10 09 08 07 06

Table of Contents

Published by Frank Schaffer Publications.
Copyright protected.

0-7682-3415-8
101 Easy Reading Games

Introduction

Games are a fantastic way to teach and reinforce concepts to students of all ages. The problem with many educational games is that they are too complicated and time consuming to set up and learn. They require hours of preparation and lengthy explanations to students. Something that is supposed to be fun turns out to require a lot of work.

This book addresses that problem by patterning reading games after familiar and well-loved game types, such as bingo and memory. By building on students' prior knowledge of game structure and rules, the time can be spent actually playing the games and reinforcing target concepts.

101 Easy Reading Games is broken down into ten major sections, according to game category. Game boards and activity pages are included with the game instructions, and game cards are included in many cases. These materials and ideas will provide you and your students with hour upon hour of fun reading practice.

The ten sections are letter games, matching games, bingo-type games, question and answer games, drawing games, board games, card games, cloze play, brain games, and moving games.

Play the matching games like traditional Memory, with cards set up facedown in a grid. Players play to see who can make the most matches.

Play the bingo games as you do any other bingo game. You may want to laminate bingo boards for repeated use, and use paper or plastic chips as the bingo markers. Within this section are also games like bingo, such as tic-tac-toe. They all involve using an area grid to finish the game.

The question and answer section includes games that may remind you of the game Jeopardy. You set up each Quiz Challenge game in a similar way, with a grid of questions that are worth various point values. If you plan to play this game often, you may want to prepare a permanent Quiz Challenge board for yourself in one of the following ways.

- Construct a board out of foam board and library pockets. Write "Quiz Challenge" at the top and attach a grid of pockets that is five across and six down. This will allow you to place the category titles at the top of each column of five questions. Label the library pockets with point values. You will be able to slip the cards into the pockets before each game and easily pull them out as you play.
- Purchase and set aside a cork board with push pins. Before play, write a point value on the back of each card and attach it to the board with the push pins.
- Purchase and set aside a pocket chart that has room for five columns and six rows. Make rectangular cards from construction paper that are big enough to cover the question cards, and label them with point values. This is a very convenient way to set up your board, because cards slide easily in and out of the pockets and column headings can be seen through the clear plastic

Published by Frank Schaffer Publications.
Copyright protected.

0-7682-3415-8
101 Easy Reading Games

The purpose of drawing games is to develop and demonstrate vocabulary and comprehension skills. Students will deepen their understanding of words, concepts, and story elements as they are challenged to show what they visualize when reading. These games also are a great way to address different learning styles and allow students with visual and artistic skills to shine.

The board games follow the general pattern of board games involving a game board with a start and an end, game markers for each player, and cards with questions on them. You may choose to use the game board provided in this section, make up your own, or use game boards you have from other games. The cards and instructions will work with any of these type of simple game boards and any game markers.

The card games section contains games designed to play just as the timeless classics Go Fish, War, Rummy, etc. The cards lend themselves well to many more games than there is room to list!

The cloze play games are modeled after fill-in-the-blank activities such as Mad Libs. Review word categories with students before playing, and, if you wish, make word lists for each of the categories used. Also review the meaning of context clues.

There are games in this book addressing all five of the key Reading First skills: phonemic awareness, decoding, fluency, vocabulary, and comprehension. You will find the games indexed by these skills on page 127.

You will find, with use, that *101 Easy Reading Games* will provide you and your students with many hours of reading fun!

You may use this blank set of cards to make your own game cards for any of the card games in this book.

Published by Frank Schaffer Publications.
Copyright protected.

0-7682-3415-8
101 Easy Reading Games

Letter Games

 **Timely Word Morphs**

Objective: apply knowledge of letter and sound correspondences

Materials: chalk, clock with second hand

Players: partners

Setting: at the board

Getting Ready: none

How to Play:

1. Using one of the word pairs listed below, have partners write the first word at the top of the board and the second word at the bottom of the board.
2. Tell students to change one letter in the top word to make a new word, which is written below the first word.
3. In two minutes, partners continue to change one letter in each word until they have formed the second word listed on the board. Challenge students to make as few changes as possible.
4. Partners earn one point for each change.
5. Continue play by giving students additional word pairs. The partner with the least number of points wins.

Word Morphs

cold ⟹ fail

gone ⟹ said

sled ⟹ heal

lime ⟹ cost

skit ⟹ flop

pour ⟹ ship

rest ⟹ coal

east ⟹ dare

Example:

ball

bell

belt

melt

meat

Published by Frank Schaffer Publications.
Copyright protected.

0-7682-3415-8
101 Easy Reading Games

Letter Games

2 Side-by-Side Compounds

Objective: recognize and practice using compound words

Materials: chart paper, newsprint, markers

Players: individuals

Setting: classroom

Getting Ready: Write the joined compound words listed below on chart paper. Draw a short line for each underlined letter as shown. Display the words and invite volunteers to identify the missing word. Challenge students to use both words in one sentence.

How to Play:

1. Ask students to write their own side-by-side compounds on newsprint. Remind them to write the words to fill the page.
2. Invite one student to hold up her compound. Allow the remaining students to identify the missing word.

3. The first student to correctly identify the missing word and use both words in one sentence shows his word next.

Side-by-Side Compounds

left<u>ove</u>rrun

chalk<u>boar</u>dwalk

turtle<u>neck</u>lace

fire<u>plac</u>emat

rail<u>roa</u>drunner

snow<u>ball</u>room

air<u>mail</u>box

0-7682-3415-8

Letter Games

 **Puzzled by Roots**

Objective: recognize and practice using Greek and Latin roots

Materials: chart paper, marker, dictionary, pencil, paper

Players: small groups

Setting: classroom

Getting Ready: none

How to Play:
1. Divide the class into groups of four or five.
2. Assign each group a root word.
3. Have the students look up the origin and meaning of the root in a dictionary.
4. Each student in the group chooses a word having the root. They find and record the definition. Group members stack the words from shortest to longest to make a puzzle on a separate sheet of chart paper.
5. Allow each group to share their puzzles.

Greek and Latin Roots

arch	man
aster/astr	mit
aud	path
clam/claim	port
corp	serv
cred	ten
dict	vac
graph	vis

Extension: Invite volunteers to use the words in sentences.

Example:

ped

1. p e d a l
2. b i p e d
3. p e d e s t a l
4. c e n t i p e d e
5. p e d e s t r i a n

Meaning: foot
1. A part of the bike that is pushed with the foot
2. An animal that has two feet
3. A base that a statue or vase sits on
4. An insect with many pairs of feet
5. A person who uses feet to walk

Published by Frank Schaffer Publications.
Copyright protected.

0-7682-3415-8
101 Easy Reading Games

Letter Games

 **Prefix Hangman**

Objective: recognize and practice using prefixes

Materials: paper, pencil, dictionary

Players: partners

Setting: free time

Getting Ready: none

How to Play:

1. One student chooses a word with a prefix.
2. The student draws a blank for each letter in the word.
3. The partner guesses the letters. If the guess is correct, the student writes the letter on as many lines as it belongs. If the guess is incorrect, the first student draws the parts of a stick-figure body in this order: head, body, arm, arm, leg, leg. If the figure is completed before the word is guessed, the first student chooses another word with a prefix to begin a new game. If the partner correctly guesses the word, he begins a new game.

Extension: Challenge the student who is guessing to use the word in a sentence.

Letter Games

 5 ## You Found My Word!

Objective: develop an understanding of content-related vocabulary before reading a fiction or nonfiction selection

Materials: graph paper (page 12), vocabulary words from a selection, pencil

Players: partners

Setting: in the classroom before reading a selection

Getting Ready: Compile a word list with four to six words from a selection students will read. Duplicate a sheet of graph paper for each student.

How to Play:

1. Introduce the vocabulary words and their meanings to students.
2. Have each student draw a frame to make a 10 x10-unit square on a piece of graph paper. They write the letters A through J across the top squares and the numbers 1 through 10 along the side squares.
3. Students write the vocabulary words on the paper so that one letter goes in a square. The words may be written horizontally or vertically anywhere on the paper.

4. The first player calls out a letter and number pair. If there is no letter in the square, the partner calls out a letter and number pair. If there is a letter in the square, the letter is identified, and the player calls out another pair. Once all the letters in the word are identified, the student who wrote the word says it. The partner who guessed must give the definition before the word can be crossed off.
5. Play continues until one partner identifies and defines all the words on the vocabulary list.

	A	B	C	D	E	F	G	H	I	J
1										
2	s	u	b	m	a	r	i	n	e	
3					q					
4					u					
5					a					
6					t					
7					i					
8					c					
9										
10										

Published by Frank Schaffer Publications.
Copyright protected.

0-7682-3415-8
101 Easy Reading Games

Name _____ Date _____

Graph Paper

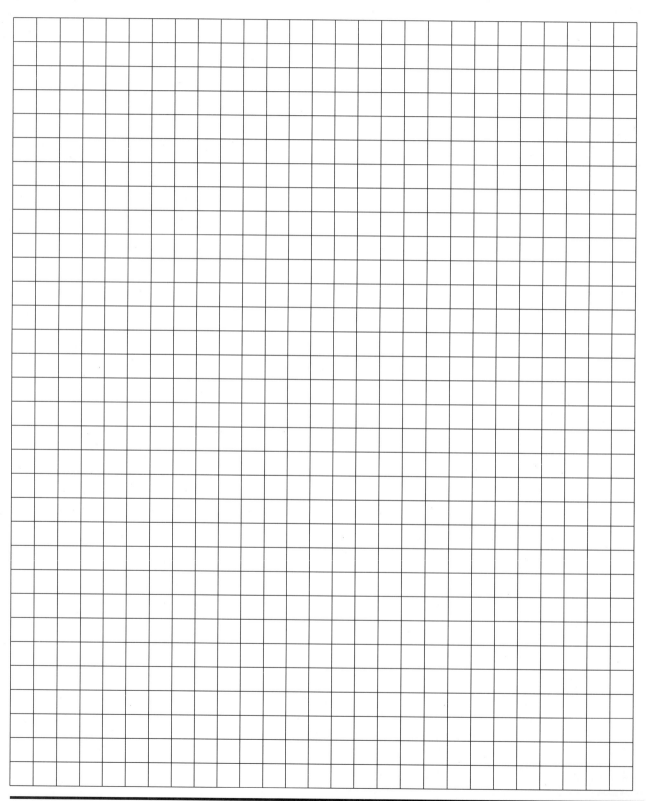

Published by Frank Schaffer Publications.
Copyright protected.

0-7682-3415-8
101 Easy Reading Games

Letter Games

6 Order in the Words, Please!

Objective: practice dictionary skills by alphabetizing words

Materials: letter tiles, two number cubes, egg timer, paper, pencil

Players: small groups

Setting: activity center

Getting Ready: none

How to Play:

1. Students place the letter tiles facedown on a table.
2. One student rolls both number cubes. This student is the lead player and turns that many tiles faceup in the middle of the group.
3. The lead player sets the egg timer for three minutes.
4. Students work individually to write down all the words they can form using those letters before the egg timer rings.
5. Group members count and compare their words. Students get a point for each word they make.
6. Students work together to help the lead player combine and alphabetize all the words into one list.
7. Play continues until each group member has had a chance to be the lead player.
8. The group member with the most overall points wins the game.

t	l	a	r	y	p	i	e	w	e

rail

real

reel

welt

wipe

Letter Games

 **Effect-ive Puzzles**

Objective: identify cause and effect

Materials: overhead projector, transparencies, transparency pens

Players: teams

Setting: classroom

Getting Ready: Prepare several transparencies that state different cause and effect relationships. Identify the cause at the top of the transparency. Draw a line for each letter of the effect at the bottom of the page. Leave a space between the words.

How to Play:

1. Divide the class into two teams.
2. On the overhead projector, display a transparency with the cause and effect relationship puzzle.
3. Have a student from team 1 guess a letter. If the guess is correct, write the letter on as many lines as it belongs. The student has one chance to guess the effect. If the guess is incorrect, team 2 gets a chance to guess a letter.
4. Play continues until the problem is solved. The team solving the puzzle earns a point.
5. The first team to earn 5 points wins.

Cause and Effect Relationships

A key turns; a door opens.

The stove gets hot; food cooks.

The phone rings; people pick up the phone.

Feet push pedals; a bike moves forward.

A finger pushes a button; a computer turns on.

Rain falls; the road gets wet.

Lights turn off; a movie starts.

An alarm clock buzzes; people wake up.

Published by Frank Schaffer Publications.
Copyright protected.

0-7682-3415-8
101 Easy Reading Games

Letter Games

Objective: identify story details

Materials: graph paper (page 12), paper, pencil

Players: individuals

Setting: free time

Getting Ready: Duplicate a sheet of graph paper for each student.

How to Play:

1. Tell students to choose a well-known character from a nursery rhyme, folk tale, or fairy tale. Have them write the name vertically on paper.

2. Challenge students to think of important details that relate to the story and contain the letters of the name. There will need to be one item for each letter in the character's name. (Some details may need to be exaggerated to include a clue for each letter.)

3. Students write the words horizontally using the letters in the name to form a puzzle.

4. On a sheet of graph paper, students outline the boxes of the puzzle, including only the letters of the character's name. They should especially darken the vertical boxes that identify the name.

5. Below the puzzle, students give clues for each horizontal item.

6. Students trade papers and solve the puzzles.

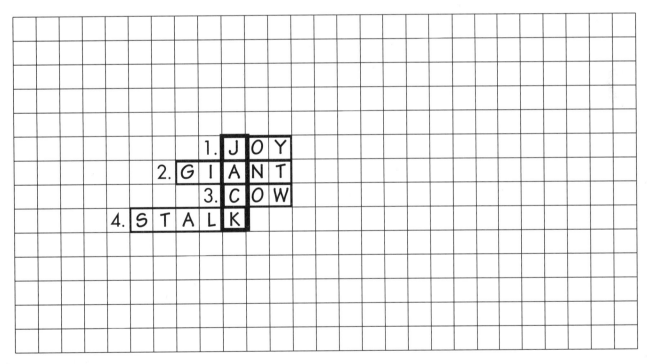

Clues:

1. The main character had this feeling when he was rich at the end of the story.
2. This character was very big.
3. This animal had to be sold.
4. The main character climbed this up into the clouds.

Letter Games

9 Wheel of Problems

Objective: recognize problems of fictional characters

Materials: point wheel (page 17), large paper clip, paper, pencil

Players: small groups of four

Setting: activity center

Getting Ready: Duplicate a point wheel and place a paper clip with the wheel.

How to Play:

1. One student is the emcee and chooses a character and problem from a familiar story. He identifies the character's name and draws a blank for each letter of the problem, leaving a space between the words.

2. Player 1 spins the wheel first. He puts the paper clip over the center dot in the wheel and puts the point of a pencil on the dot. He then spins the clip.

3. Player 1 guesses a letter. If the guess is correct, the emcee writes the letter on as many lines as it belongs, and player 1 gets the points shown on the wheel. The student has one chance to guess the problem. If he does not choose to guess, he may spin the clip again. If player 1 guesses incorrectly, player 2 repeats the process.

4. Play continues until the problem is identified. The player solving the puzzle gets to keep her points.

5. Play three more games so that each student will be the emcee. The player with the most points from all four games wins.

Jim	Colette
75	10
50	50
200	100
25	10
25	

Characters: The Three Bears

Problem: _ o l d i l o c k s
v i s i _ e d
_ h e i r h o u s e

101 Easy Reading Games

Letter Games

Point Wheel

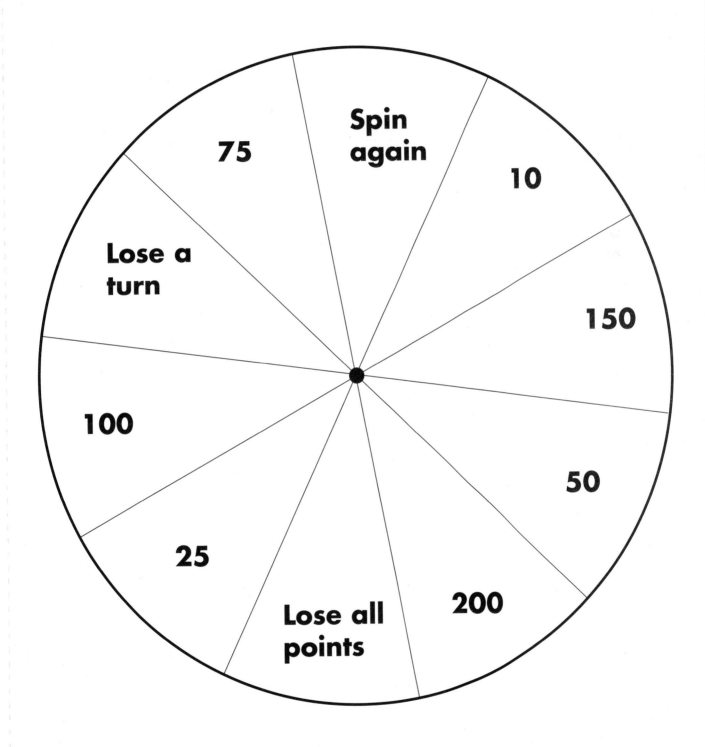

Letter Games

10 "Wheely" Funny Riddles

Objective: understand and practice using homographs

Materials: point wheel (page 17), large paper clip, pencil, marker

Players: teams

Setting: chart paper

Getting Ready: Write three of the homograph riddles below on separate sheets of chart paper. Draw a line for each letter in the answer, leaving a space between the words.

How to Play:

1. Divide the class into three teams.
2. Show students the first sheet and read aloud the riddle.
3. A player from team 1 spins the wheel first. She puts the paper clip over the center dot in the wheel and puts the point of a pencil on the dot. She then spins the clip.
4. Player 1 guesses a letter. If the guess is correct, write the letter on as many lines as it belongs, and player 1 gets the points shown on the wheel. The student has one chance to guess the inference (answer). If the guess is correct, another player from team 1 spins the wheel. If the guess is incorrect, team 2 repeats the process.
5. Play continues with teams taking turns until the riddle is solved. The team solving the puzzle gets to keep its points.
6. Play two more games. The team having the most points after all three games wins.

Homograph Riddles

Why did the businessman buy a bakery?
He wanted to make some dough.

Why did the boy pull out all of his teeth?
He wanted to chew gum.

Why did the musician go to a baseball game?
He was looking for a pitch for his song.

Why did the child climb the mountain?
He wanted to find a top.

Why did the knight raise up his hands toward the king?
He was presenting his arms.

How do giants show that they enjoy a play?
They give the actors a big hand.

Why are watermelons full of water?
They are planted in the spring.

Why did the crowd refuse to sit during the football game?
They were watching in the stands.

> How are a king and a yardstick alike?
>
> T h e y a r e r u l e r s .

Matching Games

 Possessive Memory

Objective: recognize and identify possessives

Materials: possessives memory picture cards (page 20), pocket chart, 10 index cards, markers, scissors, bag

Players: small groups

Setting: around a pocket chart

Getting Ready: Duplicate the picture cards. Cut them apart to make cards and color them if desired. Write the possessive phrases below on separate cards and put them in a bag. Place the cards in a pocket chart with the pictures hidden.

How to Play:
1. Player 1 chooses a card from the bag and reads it.
2. She turns over one card for everyone to see. If the picture matches the phrase, she keeps both cards and draws again. If the cards do not match, she returns the phrase to the bag and the card to the pocket chart.
3. Player 2 repeats the process.
4. Play continues until all pictures and phrase cards have been matched. The player with the most pairs wins.

Possessive Phrases

the dog's bone

the dog's bones

the dogs' bones

the boy's truck

the boy's trucks

the boys' truck

the boys' trucks

the baby's blanket

the babies' blanket

the babies' blankets

Alternate Version:
Write possessive phrases on paper like the picture cards, cutting them to be the same size. Allow students to independently play memory with the cards.

Published by Frank Schaffer Publications.
Copyright protected.

0-7682-3415-8
101 Easy Reading Games

Matching Games

Possessive Memory Picture Cards

Matching Games

 Pairing Up with Homophones

Objective: recognize and practice using homophones

Materials: 30 index cards, marker

Players: whole class

Setting: an area where students can walk around to find partners

Getting Ready: Write homophones on separate index cards. Each student will need one card.

How to Play:

1. Pass out the cards to students.
2. Have students walk around, quietly read the words on each other's cards, and partner with the student who has the corresponding homophone.
3. Before getting in line, challenge them to say a sentence that has both words.

Homophone Examples
(More homophones can be found on page 39.)

ad/add	in/inn
allowed/aloud	knight/night
buy/bye	mind/mined
board/bored	pail/pale
brake/break	plain/plane
flea/flee	rap/wrap
flour/flower	waist/waste
guessed/guest	way/weigh
hall/haul	whirled/world
hour/our	wood/would

crews

cruise

Published by Frank Schaffer Publications.
Copyright protected.

0-7682-3415-8
101 Easy Reading Games

Matching Games

 Rooting for the Team

Objective: recognize and identify roots in words

Materials: 24 index cards, marker

Players: small groups of three

Setting: activity center

Getting Ready: Write sets of three words with the same roots on separate cards.

How to Play:

1. Students mix up the cards and lay them facedown on a table.
2. Each player turns a card faceup. If all three words belong in the same word family, the students identify the root and keep the cards. If the three cards do not match, the cards are returned facedown to their original place.
3. Play continues until all words in the same family have been found.

Root Examples

dict: predict, contradict, dictionary

duc: reduce, produce, deduce

ject: subject, project, eject

port: import, export, report

ali: alias, alibi, alien

cit: cite, incite, citation

civ: civic, civilian, civilization

dur: endure, duration, durable

fix: fix, prefix, fixture

form: uniform, formula, conform

manual	manufacture	manicure

0-7682-3415-8
101 Easy Reading Games

Matching Games

 **See and Read Words**

Objective: learn words to develop automaticity when reading

Materials: reading selection, paper, scissors, marker

Players: reading buddies

Setting: classroom

Getting Ready: none

How to Play:

1. Have reading buddies take turns reading out loud.
2. Each reading buddy listens for words that the partner cannot read smoothly or does not know. The partner lists the words on paper along with the page number on which the word is found.
3. After students have finished reading the text, each reading buddy cuts their paper into cards. She writes each listed word on two cards and mixes all the cards together.
4. One reading buddy lays her set of cards facedown on the table.
5. The partner looks for matches. When he finds a match, he looks through the text to find the sentence containing the word and reads the sentence out loud several times to develop automaticity.
6. Reading buddies switch roles so the other partner can practice saying and reading their words.

Matching Games

15 Racing Concentration

Objective: practice finding unfamiliar words in a dictionary

Materials: paper, marker, dictionaries

Players: teams

Setting: in front of the classroom

Getting Ready: Review a text for unfamiliar words or content-related words. Choose at least ten words. Write each word on two separate sheets of paper. Mix up the papers and lay them facedown on a table in equal rows. Set two dictionaries on the table.

How to Play:

1. Divide the class into two teams.
2. Invite the first player from each team to come to the table.
3. Have each player turn over a paper and read the word. If the words match, they look them up in the dictionary. The first player to read the definition earns a point for the team. If the words do not match, the words are returned to their original position on the table.
4. The next player from each team repeats the process.
5. Play continues until all sets of words have been found.
6. Conclude by reviewing the words and their meanings.

Matching Games

16 Thumbs Up for Fluency

Objective: practice fluent reading for words in a series, words in all capitals, clauses, and quotations

Materials: sentence strips, marker

Players: individuals

Setting: seated on the floor in a group

Getting Ready: Write sentences that have a matching fluency element on sentence strips. Each student will need one. Each pattern must be used at least three times.

Examples (sentences with a list of items):

Chau packed a drink, a sandwich, and an apple in her lunch.

Lori, Adam, and Ricardo walked to school.

We saw floats, bands, and large balloons in the parade.

How to Play:

1. Pass out a sentence strip to each student. Caution students to keep their strips hidden.

2. Invite a volunteer up front. Have him read his sentence strip out loud, stressing the fluency pattern in the sentence.

3. Students who think their sentence contains the same fluency pattern stand. They take turns reading their sentences out loud.

4. The other students give a thumbs-up sign if they think a sentence follows the pattern. If a majority of the students give a thumbs-up sign, the student moves to stand beside the volunteer. If a reader gets a thumbs-down sign, she sits down.

5. All standing players reveal their sentences and identify the fluency pattern they stressed. Some sentences may reflect several patterns, so make certain students state the pattern they noticed.

6. Take up the cards that match. Students holding sentences that do not match return to their seats to continue the game.

7. Play continues until all sentence strips have been matched.

"That is one BIG present," gasped Ellen.

"Come here NOW," ordered Dad.

"STOP!" yelled the police officer.

Published by Frank Schaffer Publications.
Copyright protected.

0-7682-3415-8
101 Easy Reading Games

Matching Games

 Concentrating on Antonyms

Objective: identify antonyms

Materials: index cards, markers

Players: partners

Setting: activity center

Getting Ready: Write antonyms on separate index cards. Mix the cards together.

How to Play:
1. Students lay the cards facedown on a table in equal rows.
2. Both players turn a card faceup. If the cards show an antonym match, the students remove the cards. If the cards do not match, both cards are returned facedown to their original places.
3. Each player repeats the process.
4. Play continues until all antonym pairs have been found.

Alternate Version: Players may take turns turning up two cards at a time to try to make matches. The player at the end with the most matches is the winner.

Antonym Examples

(More antonyms can be found on page 54.)

mend/break	young/old
first/last	hated/loved
remember/forget	covered/bare
show/hide	full/empty
angry/happy	happy/sad
left/right	high/low
open/close	black/white
in/out	soft/hard
up/down	live/die
work/play	always/never
silly/serious	sink/float
near/far	light/dark

large

small

Matching Games

18 Pair Compare

Objective: recognize how things are alike and different

Materials: construction paper, recycled magazines, scissors, glue

Players: partners

Setting: at the board

Getting Ready: Have students cut out a picture of an object from a magazine and glue it on a half sheet of construction paper.

How to Play:

1. Invite pairs of students to the board and ask them to share their pictures.
2. Partners work together to draw and complete a Venn diagram. Challenge them to find at least three ways the objects are alike.
3. Repeat the process by pairing students with new partners.

Published by Frank Schaffer Publications.
Copyright protected.

0-7682-3415-8
101 Easy Reading Games

Matching Games

19   What Am I?

Objective: identify main ideas and details

Materials: fiction or nonfiction text, paper, crayons, pencil, clock with a second hand

Players: individuals

Setting: after reading

Getting Ready: Invite each student to draw a picture of a person, place, or thing described in a text they are reading. Encourage them to fill the page with the picture and include as much detail as possible. Have them fold the page into eight rectangles, number the pieces sequentially, and cut them apart. Then have students number eight cards. On the back of each card, tell them to write one detail about the item that will help a reading buddy name it.

How to Play:

1. Have students find a partner.
2. Player 1 lays her picture facedown on the desk so that the numbers are showing in order. She also lays the detail cards facedown, showing the numbers in order.
3. Player 2 writes "18" on a paper to show the starting number of points.
4. Player 2 calls out a number of a detail card.
5. Player 1 turns over the card and reads the detail out loud.
6. Player 2 has ten seconds to guess the item. If there is no guess or the guess is incorrect, player 2 deducts one point. Player 2 can choose to have the same numbered piece in the picture turned over. Again, player 2 has ten seconds to guess the item. If there is no guess or the guess is incorrect, player 2 loses another point.
7. Play continues until player 2 correctly guesses the item.
8. Partners switch roles. The student with the most points wins.

Published by Frank Schaffer Publications.
Copyright protected.

0-7682-3415-8
101 Easy Reading Games

Matching Games

 **Sequence Teamwork**

Objective: identify sequence

Materials: pocket chart, fairy tale sequence cards (pages 30–31), construction paper, markers, scissors

Players: small groups of three

Setting: around a pocket chart

Getting Ready: Duplicate the sequence cards on construction paper. Cut apart the cards and color the pictures if desired.

How to Play:

1. Have players review the four stories and the cards to become familiar with the sequences.
2. Students mix the cards together and place them in the pocket chart. Card should be turned so pictures don't show, arranged in an even grid.
3. Player 1 turns a card around.
4. Player 2 and player 3 repeat the process.
5. To claim a set, all three cards must belong to the same story and be revealed in sequential order.
6. The game continues until the group has turned around all the cards.

Alternate Version: Players may lay cards facedown on a flat surface rather than in a pocket chart. Have students take turns flipping over three cards at a time to try to reveal a sequenced set. When a player makes a correct set in the right order, he keeps that set. The player with the most cards at the end wins.

Matching Games

Fairy Tale Sequence Cards

Published by Frank Schaffer Publications.
Copyright protected.

0-7682-3415-8
101 Easy Reading Games

Matching Games

Fairy Tale Sequence Cards

The Three Billy Goats Gruff		
Goldilocks		

Published by Frank Schaffer Publications.
Copyright protected.

0-7682-3415-8
101 Easy Reading Games

Bingo Games

 Blends and Digraphs Bingo

Objective: apply knowledge of letter and sound correspondences

Materials: bingo board (page 33), index cards, bag, marker, pencil, counters or paper covers

Players: individuals

Setting: classroom

Getting Ready: Duplicate a bingo board for each student. Pass out the boards and tell students to write the following headings in the following order above each column: *l* blends, *s* blends, *r* blends, three-letter blends, and consonant digraphs (beginning and ending). Have students write words containing the patterns in the corresponding columns. Each

word should use a slightly different pattern (e.g., br, cr, dr, fr, gr). On separate index cards, write the headings and words below. Put them in a bag.

How to Play:
1. Pull a card out of the bag and call the heading and the word. Lay it faceup on the table.
2. Students cover the word that has the matching consonant sound.
3. Continue play until one student covers five words in a row, column, or diagonal. The student calls out his words to check accuracy.
4. The winner calls the words on the next game.

l blends: block, clap, flag, glass, plane, sled

r blends: bread, crow, dress, frog, grape, pretzel, train

s blends: scale, skunk, smoke, snake, spoon, stove, swim

three-letter blends: shrimp, splash, spring, square, string, throne

consonant digraphs: chair, shell, whale, thumb, duck, gold, milk, stamp, hand, ring, sink, tent, dish, test

l blends	r blends	s blends	3-letter blends	consonant digraphs
blue	bridge	score	shrub	chain
globe	grill	skate	split	ship
plane	tree	free	straw	whistle
fly	crib	sweep	squirrel	brush
sleep	drum	spot	spread	lamp

0-7682-3415-8
101 Easy Reading Games

Bingo Games

Bingo Board

		free		

Published by Frank Schaffer Publications.
Copyright protected.

0-7682-3415-8
101 Easy Reading Games

Bingo Games

22 Prefix Bingo

Objective: understand and practice using prefixes

Materials: bingo board (page 33), index cards, bag, marker, pencil, counters or paper chips

Players: individuals

Setting: classroom

Getting Ready: Duplicate a bingo board for each student. Pass out the boards and choose five prefixes that students write as headings. Help students brainstorm five words (four in the center column) that have the corresponding beginnings. As students write the selected words anywhere in the column,

you write each word's definition on an index card. Mix the cards together and lay them facedown on a table.

How to Play:

1. Turn over the top card and read the definition.
2. Have students identify the prefix category under which the word would be found.
3. Students cover the word on their game board.
4. Play continues until one student covers five words in a row, column, or diagonal. The student calls out her words to check accuracy.
5. The winner calls the definitions on the next game.

re-	un-	pre-	dis-	mis-
renew	unhappy	preview	disagree	misuse
review	untrue	prepare	disobey	misbehave
replace	unknown	**free**	disappear	mistreat
recall	unpack	pretest	disable	misspell
retell	unwrap	prewash	dislike	misunderstand

Bingo Games

 The Plural Connection

Objective: identify and practice using plurals

Materials: two colors of self-stick notes, index cards, markers, chalk, chalkboard

Players: teams

Setting: around the board

Getting Ready: Draw a large 8 x 8-unit grid on the board. Write the singular words from the chart below on index cards. Mix the cards together.

How to Play:

1. Divide the class into two teams. Gather them around the board. Place the cards facedown on a table near the board.
2. Have team 1 choose a color of self-stick notes. Team 2 gets the second color.
3. Have both teams sit in a line near the chart paper. Remind students that they should try to block the other team to keep them from the goal of four self-stick notes in a row, column, or diagonal.
4. The first student from team 2 stands and draws a card. She reads it and writes the plural anywhere on the chalkboard. If the plural is correct, the student puts a self-stick note anywhere on the 8 x 8 chart. If it is incorrect, the student sits down.
5. The first student on team 1 stands. If the player on team 2 misspelled the word, he attempts to spell it. If the team 2 player spelled the word correctly, the student from team 1 draws another card and repeats the process.
6. Play continues until one team gets four self-stick notes in a row, column, or diagonal.

Nouns and Their Plurals				
Add -s Plurals	**Add -es Plurals**	**Add -s to Plurals ending in y**	**Add -ies to Plurals ending in y following a consonant**	**Add -es to Plurals ending with /f/**
banana ⇒ bananas	gas ⇒ gases	pay ⇒ pays	fly ⇒ flies	life ⇒ lives
girl ⇒ girls	dress ⇒ dresses	tray ⇒ trays	spy ⇒ spies	knife ⇒ knives
toy ⇒ toys	coach ⇒ coaches	key ⇒ keys	try ⇒ tries	wife ⇒ wives
dog ⇒ dogs	brush ⇒ brushes	turkey ⇒ turkeys	puppy ⇒ puppies	calf ⇒ calves
tool ⇒ tools	wax ⇒ waxes	relay ⇒ relays	country ⇒ countries	wolf ⇒ wolves
hat ⇒ hats	fox ⇒ foxes	valley ⇒ valleys	party ⇒ parties	leaf ⇒ leaves
piano ⇒ pianos	buzz ⇒ buzzes	chimney ⇒ chimneys	city ⇒ cities	shelf ⇒ shelves
fork ⇒ forks	watch ⇒ watches	monkey ⇒ monkeys	mystery ⇒ mysteries	scarf ⇒ scarves
shoe ⇒ shoes	wish ⇒ wishes	alley ⇒ alleys	dictionary ⇒ dictionaries	wharf ⇒ wharves

Published by Frank Schaffer Publications.
Copyright protected.

0-7682-3415-8
101 Easy Reading Games

Bingo Games

 **Fact-oring in the Opinions**

Objective: recognize facts and opinions

Materials: graph paper (page 12), index cards, reading selection, pencil

Players: partners

Setting: at desks

Getting Ready: Ask each student to review a selection to find one fact and one opinion. Have the students write each fact and opinion on separate cards. Collect the cards and mix them up. Duplicate the graph paper. Have pairs of students outline a 6 x 6-unit grid on the graph paper.

How to Play:

1. Choose and read a card out loud.
2. Player 1 whispers to the partner if the statement is a fact or an opinion.
3. You tell the answer out loud to the class. If player 1 is correct, she writes her initials in any square in the 6 x 6-unit grid. If player 1 is not correct, player 2 writes his initials in any square.
4. Read another statement that reflects a fact or opinion. Player 2 whispers the answer.
5. You tell the answer. If player 2 is correct, he writes his name in any square. If player 2 is not correct, player 1 writes her name in any square.
6. Play continues until one of the players has initialed four squares in a row, column, or diagonal.

Bingo Games

25 Suffix Squares

Objective: identify and define words that have suffixes

Materials: dot game board (page 38), paper, pencil

Players: partners

Setting: activity center

Getting Ready: Duplicate the dot game board.

How to Play:

1. Each player chooses a different suffix, such as -ly, -ful, or -ness.

2. Players take turns drawing a line. When a player draws a line that completes a box, he says and spells a word that contains his chosen suffix. If correct, the player writes the word in the box. He gets to go again. If incorrect, the other player can say and spell a word, writing a word with her suffix in the box.

3. Play continues until all the boxes are formed. The person whose suffix appears most often wins.

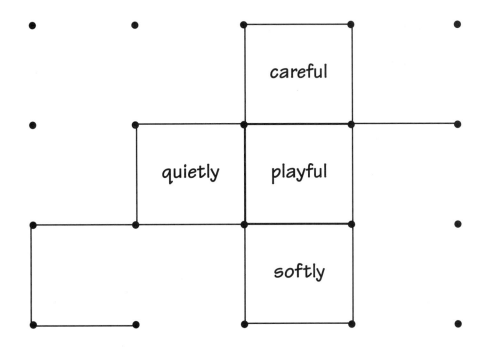

Dot Board

Bingo Games

 **Four-Corners for Homophones**

Objective: identify and practice using homophones

Materials: dot game board (page 38), pencil

Players: partners

Setting: free time

Getting Ready: Duplicate the dot game board. Draw a frame around a 6 x 4-unit board. Write a word that has a homophone in each square.

How to Play:

1. Players take turns drawing a line. When they draw a line that completes a box, they read the word, spell the corresponding homophone, and use both words in a sentence. If the answer is correct, the player writes his name in the box and gets to go again. If the answer is incorrect, the other player can spell the homophone and say a sentence using both words. If the answer is correct, the player can write her name in the box.

2. Play continues until all the boxes are formed. The person whose name appears most often wins.

Homophone Examples
(More homophones can be found on page 21.)

air/heir	maid/made
aisle/isle	mail/male
base/bass	missed/mist
blew/blue	one/won
cents/sense	peace/piece
fair/fare	road/rode
feat/feet	sail/sale
hair/hare	seam/seem
hoarse/horse	side/sighed
hole/whole	tail/tale
knew/new	wait/weight
know/no	weak/week

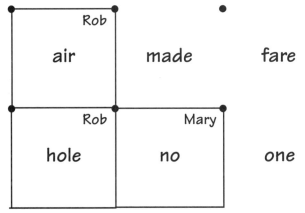

Bingo Games

 **Triangle Syllables**

Objective: recognize and identify syllables

Materials: construction paper, scissors, marker, number cube

Players: partners

Setting: activity center

Getting Ready: Cut out 21 triangles. Triangles should be at least two inches on each side. Write the words to the right on separate triangles. On the back, write the number that tells how many syllables the word has.

How to Play:

1. Have students lay the triangles faceup to form a triangle shape. There should be six triangles on the bottom row, five triangles on the second row, and so on.
2. Player 1 rolls the number cube. She picks up and reads a word with that many syllables. She keeps the triangle. If all the words with that many syllables are taken, the player forfeits her turn.
3. Player 2 repeats the process.
4. The player who picks up the last triangle wins.

Words with one syllable
store, share

Words with two syllables
country, planet, angry

Words with three syllables
hamburger, neighborhood, nutrients, another

Words with four syllables
photography, necessary, responsible, explanation

Words with five syllables
immediately, unbelievable, approximately, unpredictable

Words with six syllables
autobiography, intercontinental, unprofessionally, internationally

Published by Frank Schaffer Publications.
0-7682-3415-8
101 Easy Reading Games

Bingo Games

 "Tri" These Synonyms

Objective: recognize and identify synonyms

Materials: construction paper, scissors, marker

Players: partners

Setting: activity center

Getting Ready: Cut out 21 triangles. Triangles should be at least two inches on each side. Write a different synonym on each triangle.

How to Play:
1. Have students lay the triangles faceup to form a triangle shape. There should be six triangles on the bottom row, five triangles on the second row, and so on.
2. Player 1 tells how many triangles he will take from a horizontal row. Then he reads the words on that many triangles and names a synonym for each word. If he is correct, player 1 keeps all the triangles. If even one word is incorrect, he returns the triangles to their original position.
3. Player 2 repeats the process.
4. The player who picks up the last triangle loses.

Synonym Examples
(More Synonyms can be found on page 67.)

beautiful	cut
break	coat
brave	scared
bad	fast
small	stir
fall	happy
gather	talk
big	pick
lake	gift
find	see
smart	funny
eat	cook

Bingo Games

29 Vocabulary Cover-Up

Objective: develop an awareness of content-related vocabulary

Materials: paper, pencil

Players: individuals

Setting: on a field trip

Getting Ready: On the board, write nine content-related words that students might see or hear on the field trip. Have students fold a paper to make nine equal squares and write a word in each section.

How to Play:

1. Have students mark off each word on their game board as they hear or see it, noting where they saw it or who said it.
2. Award a prize or privilege to the first student to identify that all the words have been noticed, providing he can back up each word with a true evidence of who used the word or where it was seen.

Published by Frank Schaffer Publications.
Copyright protected.

0-7682-3415-8
101 Easy Reading Games

Bingo Games

 Author's Purpose Tic-Tac-Toe

Objective: identify author's purpose

Materials: chalk

Players: partners

Setting: at the board

Getting Ready: none

How to Play:

1. Have partners gather at the board and draw a tic-tac-toe board. They decide who will draw the X and who will draw the O.
2. Read a statement that reflects an author's purpose.
3. Player 1 whispers to the partner if the statement entertains, informs, persuades, or expresses. If the answer is correct, the player makes her mark on the board. If the answer is incorrect, no mark is made.
4. Read another statement.
5. Player 2 repeats the process.
6. Play continues until one player gets three symbols across, down, or diagonal.

Author's Purpose Examples

Entertains

Elmore put on his ski coat and his swimsuit. Now he was ready to go to school.

Jabelle picked flowers for her mother. They would be a perfect gift for her birthday.

Informs

Many artists use oil paints on a canvas.

The long ears of a jackrabbit help it hear sounds from far away.

Persuades

You should visit Pizza Party Restaurant because it serves the best pizza.

Endangered animals need our help.

Expresses

The rain beat a steady tippity-tap on the roof.

The wind swirled and whirled through the trees, making the leaves dance to the ground.

Published by Frank Schaffer Publications.
Copyright protected.

0-7682-3415-8
101 Easy Reading Games

Bingo Games

 Syllable Drop

Objective: identify sounds of syllables

Materials: none

Players: individuals

Setting: waiting in line

Getting Ready: none

How to Play:

1. Say a word with at least three syllables and have the student repeat the word.
2. Tell the students to say the word again but without a syllable you identify.

Examples

Teacher: Say the word "applesauce."

Student: *applesauce*

Teacher: Say it again, but don't say "ap."

Student: *plesauce*

Teacher: Say the word "plentiful."

Student: *plentiful*

Teacher: Say it again, but don't say "ti."

Student: *plenful*

Bingo Games

32 — What Am I? Rhyming Ladders

Objective: identify rhyming words

Materials: rhyming dictionary or Web site, chalk

Players: small groups

Setting: at the board

Getting Ready: Choose several words that have at least ten rhyming words, some of which have more than one syllable.

How to Play:

1. Form groups of three and gather at the board.
2. Tell each group to draw a ladder with ten rungs.
3. Give a riddle clue about a base word that has many rhymes, such as "I have limbs and am covered in bark. What am I?" (tree) Clap ten times slowly as a timer.
4. Have each group write the word on the bottom rung within the time limit. Check to make sure each group writes the correct word.
5. Continue to say riddles for nine other words that rhyme with the base word. Group members work together to identify the word and write it above the base word within the ten-clap time limit.
6. Groups get a point for each word they write.
7. Continue playing the game by giving students additional words. The group with the most points wins.

"Tree" Ladder

I make sure that sports teams play fairly. (referee)

I am a subject for past events. (history)

I tell you how to cook food. (recipe)

I mean that you and I think the same way. (agree)

I am a part of your body. (knee)

I give wet waves. (sea)

I don't cost a penny. (free)

I open doors. (key)

I buzz on by when I fly. (bee)

I have limbs and am covered in bark. (tree)

33 — What Am I? Rhymes

Objective: recite rhymes chorally

Materials: completed rhyme ladders from above, paper, pencil

Players: small groups from What Am I? Rhyming Ladders

Setting: classroom

Getting Ready: Have students copy one of the rhyme ladders you identify.

How to Play:

1. Have the group members write a four to six-line rhyme using some of the words on their rhyme ladder. Rhymes can be serious or nonsensical.
2. Allow time for groups to practice saying their rhymes.
3. Invite each group to chorally recite their rhyme.

Published by Frank Schaffer Publications.
Copyright protected.

0-7682-3415-8
101 Easy Reading Games

Bingo Games

34 Detective Tales

Objective: generate questions and answers

Materials: detective notes (page 47), paper, pencil

Players: individuals

Setting: classroom

Getting Ready: Duplicate the detective notes for each student.

How to Play:

1. Have students choose a fairy tale, folk tale, or familiar story in which one character may have broken the law. For example, in the story *Goldilocks and the Three Bears*, Goldilocks entered a home illegally.

2. Tell students to think of questions they could ask the character about the crime. Have them write at least five questions on the detective sheet.

3. Have students trade detective questions with a classmate. The partner answers the questions on another sheet of paper. Answers can be serious or nonsensical.

4. The answers are returned to each detective. The detective uses the questions and answers to write a short script detailing the interrogation.

35 Detective Tales Reader's Theater

Objective: practice using the correct ending intonation for questions

Materials: completed scripts from Detective Tales

Players: partners

Setting: classroom

Getting Ready: none

How to Play:

1. Have partners imagine they are the detective and the story character chosen above. Allow them time to rehearse the script. Remind students to use proper ending intonation for questions, interjections, and statements.

2. Invite partners to do a reader's theater of their scripts in front of the class.

Detective Notes

Story _____

1.

2.

3.

4.

5.

Published by Frank Schaffer Publications.
Copyright protected.

0-7682-3415-8
101 Easy Reading Games

Bingo Games

36 Book Reporter

Objective: summarize the important elements of a story

Materials: reporter recorder (page 49), fiction books, pencil

Players: individual

Setting: library

Getting Ready: Duplicate a reporter recorder for each student.

How to Play:

1. Tell students to choose a fiction book they have read.
2. Have them use the graphic organizer to record the answers to the questions.
3. Remind students that the opening paragraph of a newspaper article always summarizes the event by answering the questions who, what, where, when, why, and how. Also, the first sentence of an article is an attention getter that makes a person want to read on. Tell students to imagine that the story really happened, and they are a news reporter on the scene. Have them use the graphic organizer to help them write a summary of the story that could appear as the first paragraph of an article.
4. Invite a volunteer to read aloud his summary. Challenge the students to guess the book.

Name _____ Date _____

Reporter Recorder

Story Title _____

Who is the main character in the story?

_____

_____

Where does the story take place?

_____

_____

When does the story take place?

_____

_____

What did the character do?

_____

_____

Why did the character do it?

_____

_____

How does the story end?

_____

_____

Published by Frank Schaffer Publications.
Copyright protected.

0-7682-3415-8
101 Easy Reading Games

Question and Answer Games

37 Category Pyramid

Objective: practice classifying skills

Materials: 6 folders, paper, stapler, pushpins, markers, tape, clock with second hand

Players: small groups of three

Setting: around a bulletin board

Getting Ready: Write a 10 on the front of each folder to show a point value. Staple the folders to the bulletin board to form a pyramid—three on the bottom, two in the middle, and one on the top. Make sure the fold of each folder faces down and the front flap can open. Hold the folders closed with pushpins. Write at least 18 category questions on separate pieces of paper and put them in a large envelope.

How to Play:

1. Have one group come to the board. Tell the group to decide who will list the objects, who will guess the category, and who will be the judge.
2. Without group members looking, the judge chooses six category questions from the envelope and tapes them inside the folders.
3. The lister sits in a chair facing the folders, while the guesser sits in a chair facing away from the board.
4. The judge reminds the group they have three minutes to guess all six categories. She then unpins a folder on the bottom row.
5. The lister names items in each category.
6. The guesser phrases the answer as a question. The judge decides if the guesser is correct. When named, the judge opens the next folder. Either the lister or guesser may

choose to skip a category and proceed.
7. The guesser earns 10 points for each category correctly guessed. She earns 100 points if she identifies all the categories in three minutes.
8. Students play the game two more times so that each person has a chance to guess.

Category Questions

What are some fruits?

What are some parts of a computer?

What do you need to bake a cake?

What are some kinds of furniture?

What are some things you write with?

What are some things that are yellow?

What are some things that you read?

What are some programs on television?

What are some kinds of birds?

What are some kinds of balls?

What can you see at a circus?

What can you wear?

Who are some famous nursery rhyme characters?

What can go on a pizza?

What are things that have wheels?

What are some toys children play with?

What are some kinds of cookies?

What are some tools?

Published by Frank Schaffer Publications.
Copyright protected.

0-7682-3415-8
101 Easy Reading Games

Question and Answer Games

38 The Process of 20 Questions

Objective: identify steps in a process

Materials: paper, pencil

Players: whole class

Setting: waiting

Getting Ready: none

How to Play:

1. Invite a volunteer to choose a process. Have him write it on paper.
2. Allow students to ask 20 questions to determine the process.
3. The student who chose the process uses tally marks to track the number of questions.
4. The student who guesses the process becomes the next player.

Published by Frank Schaffer Publications.
Copyright protected.

0-7682-3415-8
101 Easy Reading Games

Question and Answer Games

39 Story Quiz Challenge

Objective: identify story elements

Materials: chart paper, index cards, marker, tape, paper, pencil, bell

Players: reading club

Setting: around chart paper

Getting Ready: Choose five books the students have read. Write the titles on index cards. On the back of each card, write the numbers 1 to 5. Tape the cards to the chart paper as headings. The numbers should show. On index cards, write answers to questions that relate to the five story elements (character, setting, problem, event, solution) in each book. On the back of the cards, write point values of 10, 20, 30, 40, and 50. Tape the cards in the corresponding column with the points showing sequentially.

How to Play:

1. Invite three volunteers to play the game. Ask another student to tally the scores during the game.
2. Player 1 chooses a number.
3. Read the answer out loud and give the player 10 seconds to respond with the question. If player 1 answers correctly, she earns the points and may choose another card. If she answers incorrectly or you ring the bell, any player may answer and earn the points. That player also chooses the next card.
4. If no one answers correctly, player 2 chooses a card.
5. Students continue to ask and answer questions. At any time, a student may call out a number to identify the title of the book. If she is correct, the student gets 50 points. If she is incorrect, she loses 50 points.
6. The game continues until all the cards are revealed. The player with the most points wins.

Published by Frank Schaffer Publications. Copyright protected.

0-7682-3415-8
101 Easy Reading Games

Question and Answer Games

 **Questioning the Facts**

Objective: recognize facts

Materials: pocket chart, index cards, paper, pencil, 3 bells

Players: teams

Setting: in front of the pocket chart

Getting Ready: Choose six topics relating to areas of study. Write the topics on index cards. Write three sets of point values of 10, 20, 30, 40, and 50 on index cards. Place them sequentially in the pocket chart.

How to Play:

1. Divide the class into six teams. Give each team a topic card.
2. Each team writes five questions about topic-related facts on separate index cards. They write the answer on the back.
3. Have three teams come to the front of the classroom and sit in a line in front of the pocket chart. Give the first player on each team a bell.
4. Collect the cards from the other three teams. Place the topic cards as the

headings in the pocket chart. Place a question card behind each point value card.

5. Invite the first player on team 1 to choose a category and point value.
6. Read the question out loud. Only players holding a bell may answer. The first student to ring the bell and answer correctly gets the points for the team. If the student answers incorrectly, the team loses that many points. Other students holding the bell may answer after ringing it.
7. The bell is passed down the line to the next team player. The team that earned the points chooses the next category and point value. If no one answered correctly, team 2 chooses a card.
8. The game continues until all the cards are revealed. The group with the most points wins.
9. The board groups and the answering groups switch roles to play another game.

Published by Frank Schaffer Publications.
Copyright protected.

0-7682-3415-8
101 Easy Reading Games

Drawing Games

 **Antonym Pictures**

Objective: recognize antonyms

Materials: index cards, marker, chalk

Players: teams

Setting: at the board

Getting Ready: Write antonyms on index cards.

How to Play:
1. Divide the class into two teams—team A and team B.
2. One player from each team goes to the board.
3. Give the students a card. The student from team A draws a picture to illustrate the first word, and the student from team B draws a picture of the second word.
4. The first team that calls out the antonym pair earns a point for the team.
5. Play continues so that all students have an opportunity to draw at the board.

Antonym Examples

(More antonyms can be found on page 26.)

cold/hot	begin/end
long/short	fast/slow
large/small	on/off
right/wrong	hard/soft
push/pull	awake/asleep
slowly/quickly	high/low
rough/smooth	buy/sell
begin/finish	over/under
easy/hard	laughed/cried
lead/follow	whisper/shout
friend/enemy	poor/rich
quiet/loud	old/new
same/different	correct/incorrect

Published by Frank Schaffer Publications.
Copyright protected.

0-7682-3415-8
101 Easy Reading Games

Drawing Games

 **Picturing Homophones**

Objective: identify homophones

Materials: paper, crayons

Players: individuals

Setting: activity center

Getting Ready: none

How to Play:

1. Invite students to brainstorm homophones. Record the list on the board.
2. Tell students to choose a pair of words from the board, or other ones they think of, and draw a picture that shows the words. For example, students might draw a bear without fur to show the homophones "bare/bear."

3. Have students write the homophone phrase on the back.
4. Have students leave their drawings in the center for classmates to guess.

Homophone Examples

(More homophones can be found on pages 21 and 39.)

dear/deer	sea/see
flower/flour	son/sun
meat/meat	scene/seen
ring/wring	toad/towed
rose/rows	steak/stake

Drawing Games

 **43** **Drawn to Metaphors**

Objective: recognize and practice using metaphors

Materials: paper, crayons, index cards, pencil

Players: individuals

Setting: free time

Getting Ready: none

How to Play:

1. Review that a metaphor is a kind of figurative language where two unlikely objects are compared. Give the following example: *Ella had a heart of stone.*
2. Invite students to draw a picture to represent a metaphor.
3. Have them write a sentence on an index card to go along with their picture.
4. Place the pictures and cards in an activity center. Challenge students to match the cards to the pictures.

Drawing Games

 **A Picture Worth 1,000 Words**

Objective: use text features

Materials: interesting poster, mural paper, tape, marker

Players: whole class

Setting: free time

Getting Ready: Tape the poster to a wall beside the mural paper.

How to Play:
1. Explore the phrase "A picture is worth 1,000 words."
2. Direct students to look at the poster. Invite them to brainstorm a list of words that describe the picture.
3. Record the words, numbering them sequentially.
4. Invite students to continue adding words to the list in their free time and as they hear or learn new words. Challenge students to write 1,000 words.
5. After one week, review the words and discuss how pictures help explain the text, give more information, and make a story more appealing.

Published by Frank Schaffer Publications.
Copyright protected.

0-7682-3415-8
101 Easy Reading Games

Drawing Games

 **Cause and Effect Picture Chains**

Objective: identify cause and effect

Materials: mural paper, crayons

Players: small groups

Setting: classroom

Getting Ready: Cut the mural paper into three-foot lengths. Each group will need one piece of paper.

How to Play:

1. Divide the class into groups of four.
2. Have students work together to draw a picture that shows a chain of three cause and effect relationships. For example, a picture might show a boy holding a broken leash. He is looking surprised. A dog with part of leash on its collar is chasing a cat. The cat is knocking into a table from which a fish bowl is toppling.
3. Have groups share their pictures so that other students can identify the chain.

Published by Frank Schaffer Publications.
Copyright protected.

0-7682-3415-8
101 Easy Reading Games

Drawing Games

 **Picture Predictions**

Objective: make predictions

Materials: paper, pencils, scissors, bag, chalk

Players: whole class

Setting: at the board

Getting Ready: none

How to Play:

1. Invite students to choose a specific item to draw, such as a house, tree, bike, or pig.
2. Have students fold a sheet of paper into eighths and cut along the fold lines to make eight cards.
3. Tell students to think of eight parts of their chosen item. Have them write one part on each card.
4. Invite a volunteer to come to the board. Have him put his cards into a bag.
5. Ask the student to pull one card out of the bag and draw the part shown on the card. He does not reveal the word on the card.
6. The student steps back and allows the other students to predict what he is drawing.
7. The student continues the drawing process, secretly noting the first student to guess the item.
8. When the drawing is complete, he identifies the student who guessed first. The student tells what helped her make the prediction.
9. The student who makes the first correct prediction draws next.

Drawing Games

 **Picturing Details**

Objective: make mental images of a text as a way to understand process or events encountered during reading

Materials: image stories (page 61), mural paper, crayons

Players: small groups

Setting: around mural paper

Getting Ready: Provide a four-foot section of mural paper for each group.

How to Play:
1. Divide the class into small groups.
2. Read aloud one of the image stories. Suggest students get a mental picture of the action as you read to help them understand what is happening.
3. After reading the paragraph, pass out a length of mural paper to each group and have them spread out around the classroom.
4. Tell students to draw a picture of the events from the selection. Challenge them to draw as much detail as they can remember.
5. Reread the selection. Tell students to give their group a point for each detail they included in the picture.
6. Provide a small reward or privilege for the group that has the most points.

Drawing Games

Image Stories

#1

Mrs. Washington opened the door and gasped. She could not believe her eyes and ears. The small red chair was flipped over. The four couch pillows were scattered all over the room. The birdcage was opened, and her green and yellow parrot was perched on top of the curtains squawking loudly. Rufus, the sheep dog, stood on his back legs. His big paws rested on the back of the blue couch. He barked wildly at a small black kitten. The kitten's back was arched and her claws were swiping at the big, hairy dog.

"Rufus!" Mrs. Washington scolded. "What are you doing?"

#2

Ben took one more look in the mirror. He had to admit that he had outdone himself this year. His sister's pink ball cap sat inside out and backwards on his red hair. His yellow and black striped shirt was also inside out and backwards. Ben liked the way the tag showed on the collar. He thought it was a nice touch. Ben had also found a pair of pants his father had worn in the 70s. They were red and green plaid. It had been hard to put them on inside out and backwards, but Ben had worked to be successful. Yes, he would certainly win the backwards award at school this year.

Murial, Ben's sister, opened the door. "What are you wearing?" she asked. "I hope you know that Backwards Day is tomorrow!"

#3

The beach was teeming with people. A small girl in a red swimsuit sat with her mother by the water. She squealed with delight as the waves curled around her feet. A boy with brown hair grabbed his body board and dashed into the water. He could see the bigger waves just off shore and hoped to catch a few to ride in. Over in the sand two girls laughed as they constructed a sand castle. They had built three turrets around a big mound of sand. Shells and seaweed decorated their creation. Several people gathered around the girls, admiring the structure.

Drawing Games

 **Detailed Drawings**

Objective: identify details

Materials: paper, pencil, crayons

Players: individuals

Setting: field trip

Getting Ready: none

How to Play:

1. Tell students to choose one important item on the field trip. Have them note at least five details about it. Suggest they pay attention to color, position, materials, small damages, etc.

2. Once back in the classroom, invite students to draw the item, making sure to include all the details listed on their paper.

3. Invite pairs to share their drawings. Challenge the partners to note the five details.

Published by Frank Schaffer Publications.

0-7682-3415-8
101 Easy Reading Games

Drawing Games

 **Character Web Site**

Objective: recognize the story element of characters

Materials: paper, markers

Players: reading club

Setting: classroom

Getting Ready: none

How to Play:

1. Have partners chose a character from a book they recently read.
2. Invite them to design two Web site pages, the opening page and another page, for this character. Partners should include images of important items that identify the character, as well as other subtle hints, like colors and phrases, the character frequently uses. They should not put the character's name anywhere on the pages.
3. Allow partners to share their Web site pages for other reading club members to guess the character.

Published by Frank Schaffer Publications.
Copyright protected.

0-7682-3415-8
101 Easy Reading Games

Drawing Games

 **Get the Message**

Objective: identify idioms

Materials: chart paper, paper, markers, crayons, computer with Internet

Players: individuals

Setting: free time

Getting Ready: Write the two idiom messages below on chart paper.

How to Play:

1. Have students solve the picture sentences to discover the idioms.
2. Invite students to visit a Web site that lists idioms. Encourage them to learn the origin of some of the idioms they find interesting.
3. Challenge students to write their own idiom messages.
4. Have students ask a classmate to solve the idioms.

H + EEEE  + ching $\begin{array}{r} 2 \\ +2 \\ \hline 4 \end{array}$ ZZZZ

It's  + ing

Board Games

 **Racetrack Talk**

Objective: read interjections and end marks with correct intonation

Materials: game board (page 66), construction paper, marker, scissors, colored toy cars, number cube

Players: small groups

Setting: free time

Getting Ready: Duplicate a game board on construction paper. Cut blank construction paper into cards and write the sentences listed at the bottom of the page on separate cards.

How to Play:

1. Players choose a car as their playing piece and put them on START/FINISH.
2. Each player rolls the number cube. The player with the highest number goes first, followed by the player rolling the next highest number, and so on.
3. Player 1 rolls the number cube and moves that many spaces. She follows the directions on the board. If she lands on a car space, she draws a card to read. The other players judge if she reads the sentence with correct intonation. (Remind students that they are judging interjections, where the voice shows excitement, and ending marks, where the voice raises on a question, stays level on a statement and command, and shows excitement on an exclamation.) If the sentence is read incorrectly, the player moves back two spaces.
4. Cards are returned to the bottom of the deck.
5. The first player to return to START/FINISH wins the game.

Racetrack Talk Cards

The race starts in two hours.

The drivers are getting into their cars.

The car with the best trial time will get the starting position.

The pit crew can change the tire quickly.

How fast is the driver going?

What lap is the lead car on?

Why is the yellow flag out?

Do you think the number three car will win?

Wow, look how fast those cars are going!

Look out, they are going to crash!

What a close finish in that race!

Yay, my favorite driver won the race!

Published by Frank Schaffer Publications.
Copyright protected.

0-7682-3415-8
101 Easy Reading Games

Racetrack Talk Game Board

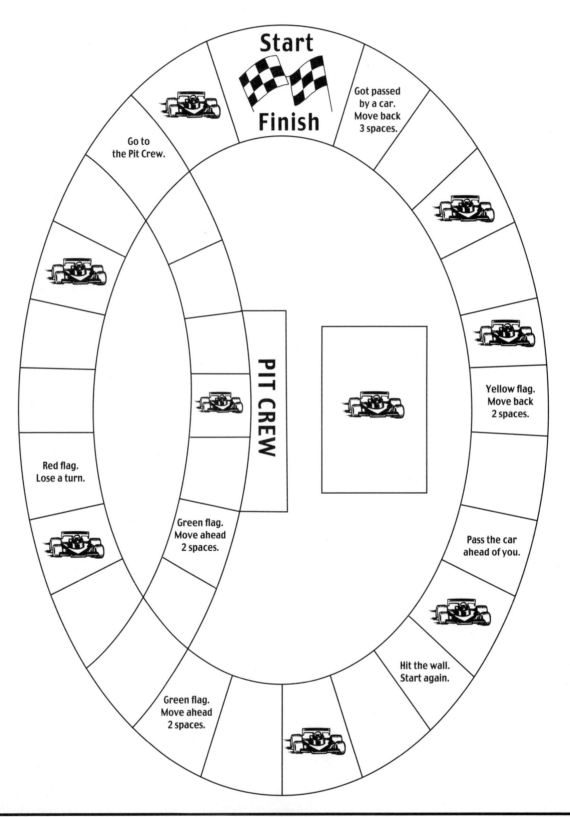

Start

Finish

Got passed
by a car.
Move back
3 spaces.

Go to
the Pit Crew.

PIT CREW

Yellow flag.
Move back
2 spaces.

Red flag.
Lose a turn.

Green flag.
Move ahead
2 spaces.

Pass the car
ahead of you.

Hit the wall.
Start again.

Green flag.
Move ahead
2 spaces.

Board Games

 **Snowboarding with Synonyms**

Objective: recognize and practice using synonyms

Materials: game board (page 68), construction paper, marker, scissors, pencil

Players: partners

Setting: free time

Getting Ready: Duplicate a game board on construction paper. Cut blank construction paper into cards and write a synonym on each.

How to Play:

1. Students mix up the cards and place them facedown on the table.
2. Player 1 draws a card and reads the word out loud. She says a synonym for the word. If her answer is correct, she writes the word on the top line on her side of the mountain. If the word is incorrect, she does not write anything.
3. Player 1 gives the card to player 2, who says another synonym of the word. If the word is correct, player 2 writes the word on the top line on his side of the mountain. If the word is incorrect, player 2 does not write anything.

4. Player 2 draws a card from the deck. He repeats the process.
5. Play continues until both players reach the bottom of the mountain.

Synonym Examples

(More Synonyms can be found on page 41.)

choose	mad
friend	pretty
happy	rabbit
hard	rug
jump	sad
large	shake
laugh	throw
little	tired
look	slow

Published by Frank Schaffer Publications.
Copyright protected.

0-7682-3415-8
101 Easy Reading Games

Snowboarding with Synonyms Game Board

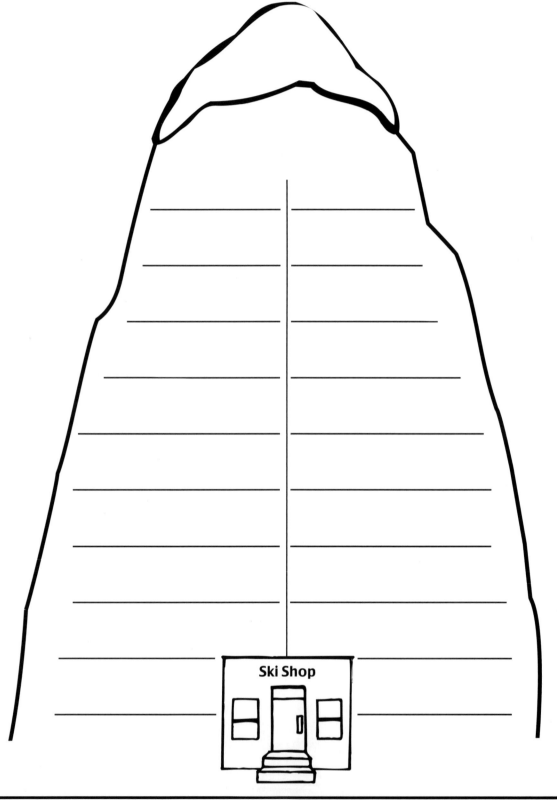

Ski Shop

Board Games

 **Making a Sound Move**

Objective: recognize and practice using onomatopoeia

Materials: game board (page 70), construction paper, counters, number cube, handled playing pieces

Players: partners

Setting: activity center

Getting Ready: Duplicate the game board on construction paper. Color the pictures if desired.

How to Play:

1. Have students cover each picture with a counter.
2. Players put their game piece on any square of the board.
3. Have player 1 roll the number cube. She moves that many squares vertically and/or horizontally.
4. Player 1 picks up the counter and says an onomatopoeia that corresponds to the picture. If the word is correct, her turn is over. If the word is incorrect, she covers the picture and stays where she is.
5. Player 2 repeats the process. However, any uncovered picture is a block and players cannot go over it or land on it. If there is no move, the player forfeits his turn.
6. Play continues until all pictures are uncovered. The player with the most counters wins.

Making a Sound Move Game Board

Board Games

 **What's Your Story?**

Objective: summarize the important elements of a story

Materials: game board (page 72), summarizing graphic organizer (page 73), markers, color counters, pencil, number cube

Players: small groups of three

Setting: activity center

Getting Ready: Duplicate the game board and color the squares if desired. Duplicate copies of the summarizing graphic organizer.

How to Play:

1. Players choose a counter color as their playing piece and put the counters on START.
2. Each student chooses a familiar story and completes the graphic organizer about the important details. They do not share the name of the story.

3. Players take turns rolling the number cube. The player with the highest number goes first, followed by the player rolling the next highest number, and so on.
4. Player 1 rolls the number cube and moves that many spaces. She reads the word and can ask either player to tell the detail that relates to his story. (For example: if the player lands on the word "who," she asks player 3 to tell who is the most important character in the book. Player 3 must answer honestly.) All players can take notes about the answers.
5. When a player knows the books of the other players, she must say the titles and summarize the stories, telling, who, what, where, when, and why, in order to win the game. An incorrect answer will mean that the player is eliminated.

Name _____ Date _____

What's Your Story Game Board

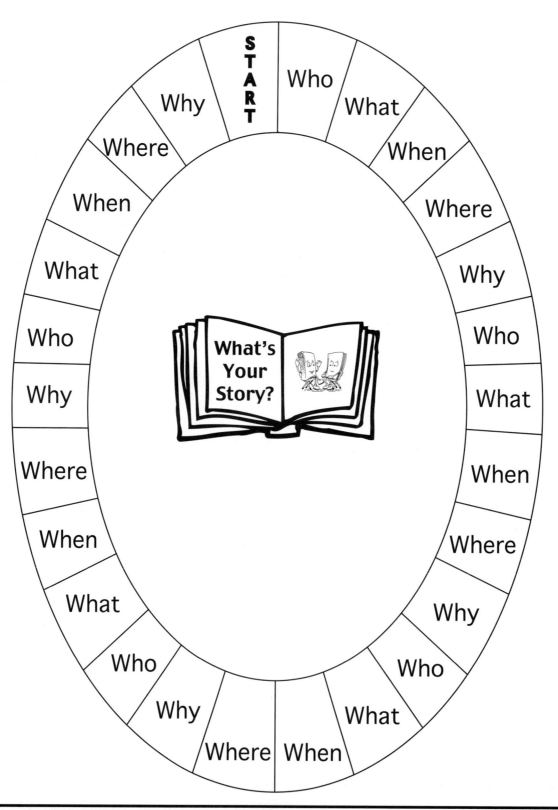

Published by Frank Schaffer Publications.
Copyright protected.
0-7682-3415-8
101 Easy Reading Games

Name _____ Date _____

Summarizing Graphic Organizer

Story Title _____

Who	**What**
Where	**When**

Why

Published by Frank Schaffer Publications.
Copyright protected.

0-7682-3415-8
101 Easy Reading Games

Board Games

55 Check Out What You Know

Objective: identify prior knowledge

Materials: game board (page 75), two colors of counters

Players: reading buddies

Setting: prior to reading a selection

Getting Ready: Duplicate the game board. Review the text to identify the topic for students to think about.

How to Play:
1. Players choose a counter color and set up the board to play checkers.
2. Players follow the rules of checkers. However, when a player jumps, he must state something he knows related to the topic.
3. The player with the last counter on the board wins.

Name _____ Date _____

Check Out What You Know Game Board

Board Games

56 Booked for a Vacation

Objective: identify parts of a book

Materials: game board (page 77), construction paper, color counters, number cube, nonfiction book

Players: small groups

Setting: free time

Getting Ready: Duplicate the game board on construction paper. Color the board if you wish.

How to Play:

1. Players choose a counter color as their playing piece and put the counters on HOME.
2. Players take turns rolling the number cube. The player with the highest number goes first, followed by the player rolling the next highest number, and so on.
3. Player 1 rolls the number cube and moves that many spaces. To enter a site, the player must roll the exact number.
4. When a player enters a site, she finds that part of the book and signs her initials on the board. The player may pass through a site.
5. The first player to visit all the vacation sites wins.

Published by Frank Schaffer Publications.
Copyright protected.

0-7682-3415-8
101 Easy Reading Games

Booked for a Vacation Game Board

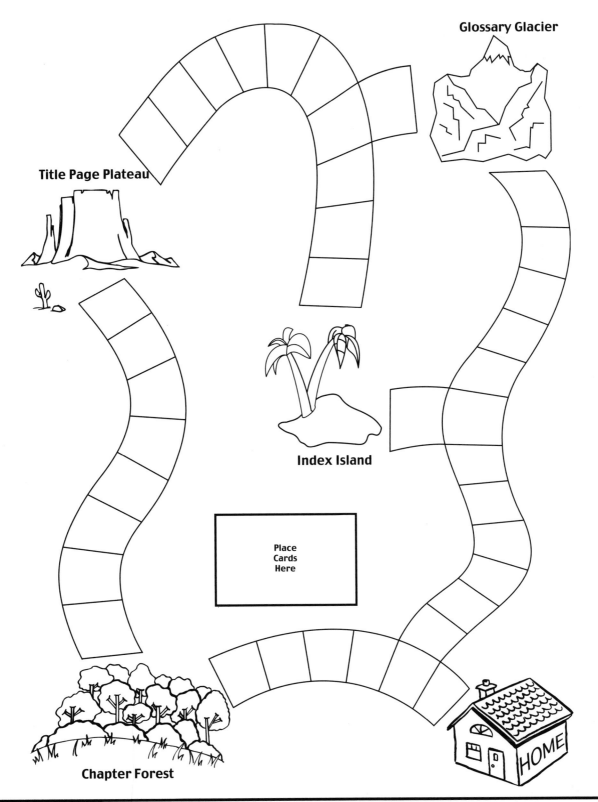

Glossary Glacier

Title Page Plateau

Index Island

Place
Cards
Here

Chapter Forest

HOME

Card Games

57 Fishing for Synonyms

Objective: identify synonyms

Materials: construction paper, scissors, marker

Players: small groups of three

Setting: activity center

Getting Ready: Write the synonyms listed on separate cards. Mix the cards together.

How to Play:

1. Students deal five cards facedown. The rest of the cards are placed facedown in the center of the table.
2. Players pick up their cards and look for synonym matches. When they get a pair, players lay the two cards faceup on the table.
3. Player 1 chooses one of the other players and says a synonym.
4. If the player has a corresponding synonym, he gives it to player 1. If not, player 1 must draw from the deck. When a player makes a pair, he lays the two cards down.
5. The game continues with players taking turns asking for cards.
6. The player who gets rid of all his cards first wins.

Synonyms

beautiful, gorgeous

crack, shatter

brave, daring

terrible, horrible

questioned, queried

active, busy

tiny, minute

smart, intelligent

fall, tumble

eat, gobble

cut, chop

coat, jacket

scared, terrified

quick, speedy

stir, mix

eager, willing

talk, speak

pick, select

gift, present

study, examine

funny, hilarious

identify, name

Card Games

58 New Word Match-Up

Objective: develop an understanding of content-related vocabulary before reading a fiction or nonfiction selection

Materials: index cards, markers

Players: small groups

Setting: before reading a selection

Getting Ready: Compile a word list with 15 words from a selection students will read. Write the words and their phonetic spellings on separate cards. Draw a picture of a dictionary on another card. Mix the cards together.

How to Play:

1. Students deal out all the cards facedown.
2. Players pick up their cards and lay down the cards that have a word and matched phonetic respelling. They say a sentence using the word.
3. The game continues like Old Maid, with the dictionary being the card that does not have a match. Player 1 can pick a card from another player without looking. If there is a match, the player can put the cards down and use the word in a sentence. If there is no match, player 2 picks a card.
4. The game continues until all the matches have been made. The player holding the dictionary card deals the cards for the next game.
5. The student with the most pairs of cards wins.

Published by Frank Schaffer Publications.
Copyright protected.

0-7682-3415-8
101 Easy Reading Games

Card Games

59 Alpha Order

Objective: practice dictionary skills by alphabetizing words to the fifth letter

Materials: index cards, markers

Players: partners

Setting: activity center

Getting Ready: Make two sets of the words in the chart. Keep the cards in separate sets.

How to Play:

1. Have each student shuffle a set of cards. Cards should remain facedown in a deck.
2. One player says "go."
3. Both players turn the top five cards faceup.
4. The players alphabetize each set of cards.
5. The player who finishes ordering the cards first wins the match. He puts the five cards aside. The other player shuffles the cards back into the set.
6. The player who gets rid of all the cards first wins.

Word List

(You may add words or change the words to fit vocabulary skill needs.)

brace	bridge
braid	bridle
brain	brief
brake	bright
branch	bring
brand	brink
brass	brisk
brave	broad
bread	broil
break	broke
breath	bronze
breeze	broom
bribe	brown
brick	browse
bride	brush

Published by Frank Schaffer Publications.
Copyright protected.

0-7682-3415-8
101 Easy Reading Games

Card Games

60   Antonym Puzzle

Objective: identify antonyms

Materials: antonym puzzle (page 82), construction paper, scissors, envelope

Players: individuals

Setting: free time

Getting Ready: Duplicate the puzzle on construction paper for each child. Cut the cards apart and place them in an envelope.

How to Play:

1. Challenge the student to put the 12 puzzle pieces back together so that the antonyms match.

Card Games

Antonym Puzzle

brave	smooth	rough
laugh	interested bored	after before shout
cold	begin	lead
hot	finish	follow
cry	slow fast	bottom top whisper
long	true	float
short	false	sink
push	right wrong	different same poor
large	easy	quiet
small	hard	loud
pull	all nothing	worst best rich
curve	straight	scared

Published by Frank Schaffer Publications.
Copyright protected.

0-7682-3415-8
101 Easy Reading Games

Card Games

61 Classified Groups

Objective: practice classifying skills

Materials: four colors of construction paper, recycled catalogs, scissors, glue

Players: small groups (2–4 players)

Setting: activity center

Getting Ready: Cut the construction paper into 2-inch x 3-inch cards. You will need 10 cards of each color. Choose 10 categories of different items, such as shoes, tools, food, phones, lamps, plants, etc. Cut out four pictures that belong in each category. Glue the pictures in a category to a different card color. (A shoe will be glued on a red, yellow, blue, and green card.) Mix the cards together.

How to Play:

1. Have a player deal seven cards facedown to each player. The remaining cards in the deck are placed facedown in the middle of the table. The top card is turned faceup.
2. Have students pick up their cards and look at them.
3. Player 1 discards a card. The card must either be the same color or in the same category as the one facing up on the table. If the player does not have a card to get rid of, she picks from the deck. If the card is the same color or the same category, she may discard this card. Otherwise, she adds the card to her hand.
4. The other players, taking turns, repeat the process. When there are no cards left in the deck, the discard pile is shuffled and becomes the deck.
5. The first player to get rid of all her cards wins.

Published by Frank Schaffer Publications.
Copyright protected.

0-7682-3415-8
101 Easy Reading Games

Card Games

 **Building a Group Story**

Objective: recognize story elements

Materials: construction paper, marker, paper, pencil

Players: small groups

Setting: gathered together while seated on the floor

Getting Ready: Cut construction paper into quarters to make cards. Write the details of the elements below on separate cards. Write "Solution" on ten cards. Include other ideas if you would like. Mix the cards together.

How to Play:

1. Divide the class into groups of four.
2. Deal out five cards facedown to each group. The rest of the cards are turned facedown in the center of the floor.
3. Each group looks at its cards. The object is to get a card with each story element.
4. Group 1 discards a card that it does not want and chooses one from the deck.
5. Group 2 discards a card that it does not want. The group can choose the card that Group 1 discarded or choose one from the deck.
6. Play continues with each group discarding a card and picking one from the deck or discard pile. If the deck runs out of cards, shuffle the discard pile and turn it facedown on the table to continue the game.
7. When groups get all five elements, have them move away and plan a story using the elements shown on the cards. Stories can be serious or nonsense.
8. Have groups share their cards and stories with the class.

Character	Setting	Problem	Event
Muscles, the mouse	farm	loses something	goes somewhere
Chester, the dog	mall	needs something	meets someone
Misha, a horse	store	finds something	finds something
Tia, an elf	park	is lost	eats something
Olive, a talking flower	racetrack	scared to be alone	grows something
Baxter, a race car	computer land	unhappy about something	makes something
Mr. Ramos, a storeowner	space	is lost	asks a friend
Renee, a champion skateboarder	sea	something breaks	searches for something
Lee, a computer gamer	city	something is missing	hides something
Captain Doran, space explorer	library	needs to go somewhere	sees something

Solution

Write "solution" on ten cards. Groups will be responsible for coming up with their own solutions.

Published by Frank Schaffer Publications.
Copyright protected.

0-7682-3415-8
101 Easy Reading Games

Card Games

63 Order Sorter

Objective: recognize the sequence of events

Materials: fairy tale sequence cards (pages 30–31), construction paper, markers (optional), scissors

Players: partners

Setting: free time

Getting Ready: Duplicate two sets of the sequence cards on construction paper. Color them if desired. Cut the cards apart. Keep the cards in separate decks.

How to Play:

1. Have players review the five stories and the cards to become familiar with the sequences. Tell them the object of the game is to line up the cards in order to show the events in a story.

2. Each player holds a deck facedown and shuffles their cards.

3. Then one player says "go." Both players turn the cards faceup one at a time as fast as they can. When finding the first card in a sequence, a player lays it faceup on the table. The other cards are discarded in a pile.

4. Players continue to flip cards and build the pictures of story sequences in order. When a player is out of cards, she picks up the discard pile, turns it facedown, and begins turning cards again.

5. The player who gets all six stories with the three cards in sequential order wins.

Published by Frank Schaffer Publications.
Copyright protected.

0-7682-3415-8
101 Easy Reading Games

Card Games

 **What Would You Say, Dear?**

Objective: practice using the intonation and expression of story characters

Materials: fairy tale sequence cards (pages 30–31), construction paper, markers (optional), scissors, pocket chart

Players: individuals

Setting: Invite students who are waiting for other class members to complete a task to play this game during the course of a day.

Getting Ready: Duplicate the sequence cards on construction paper. Color them if desired. Cut the cards apart.

How to Play:

1. Have students choose a card and say a sentence that one of the characters might say during that part of the story. Challenge them to use the intonation and expression appropriate to the character and situation.
2. Invite other students to guess the story and event.
3. Students categorize and sequence the cards in a pocket chart as they are revealed.

Published by Frank Schaffer Publications.
Copyright protected.

0-7682-3415-8
101 Easy Reading Games

Card Games

65 Racing to Compare

Objective: recognize how things are alike

Materials: index cards, recycled catalogs, scissors, glue

Players: teams

Setting: classroom

Getting Ready: Cut out simple pictures of objects such as toys, animals, vehicles, or furniture from catalogs. Try to get a wide variety of items from many categories. Make enough cards so that each student will get three cards. Glue the pictures on separate index cards. Mix the cards together.

How to Play:

1. Select two referees. Divide the rest of the class into two teams. Have each team sit side by side on the floor. Both teams should face each other. One referee stands at the beginning of the line.
2. Ask the referees to place one picture card facedown in front of each student. Students may not look at their cards.
3. One referee says "go." The referees give a card faceup to the first student in their line.
4. The student flips his card faceup. He must state a characteristic that both pictures have in common. Characteristics can include obvious similarities (They are both round.) to subtle similarities (Both names have a long o vowel sound.) If the referee agrees, she says "go."
5. The first player picks either card and hands it to the next student in line. That student flips over her card and states a characteristic that the pictures have in common. If players cannot find a way the items are the same, they say "pass."
6. The game continues with each team comparing the pairs of cards as quickly as they can. The first team to have all members participate yells "done." The other team must stop.
7. The referee gives a point to the team for each correct comparison and records the score.
8. The referees gather the cards, shuffle them together, and redistribute the cards to play again.

Published by Frank Schaffer Publications.

0-7682-3415-8
101 Easy Reading Games

Card Games

66 **Field Trip Summary**

Objective: practice summarizing

Materials: index cards, marker (or use cards below)

Players: whole class

Setting: before leaving the field trip site

Getting Ready: Write the following question words on cards: *who, what, where, when, how, why.* Make several sets so that each student can get a card. Mix the cards together and take them on the field trip.

How to Play:
1. Have students choose a card.
2. On a signal from you, have students quickly form groups of six. Each group should have a question word.
3. Visit each group. Have them summarize the field trip before boarding the bus to return to school.

who	what	where
when	how	why

Card Games

67 Tag Team

Objective: read sentences with the correct intonation using tags

Materials: sentence strips, markers

Players: teams

Setting: classroom

Getting Ready: Write about 30 sentences with expressive tags. Some examples are given. Mix the strips together.

How to Play:

1. Divide the class into two teams.
2. Put the strips facedown on a table. Make sure that students understand that a *tag* is the word in a direct quotation that tells how the word was spoken. For example, in the sentence *"That's horrible!" groaned Oscar,* the tag is *groaned.* It shows how the character was feeling and how he may have said the sentence.
3. Invite the first player from each team to come forward. Have the two students each choose a sentence strip. Each player reads the strip with the correct expression and intonation based on the tag. Encourage students to be creative in their voice responses. If you judge the students to be fluent, the team earns a point.
4. Play continues until each team member has read a sentence.
5. Sentence strips can be reshuffled and used again.
6. The team with the most points wins.

Tag Sentences

"That was a fun ride," giggled Angie.

"You are late," Mom said sternly.

"I just won a computer!" gasped Tony.

"I have three books to check out," whispered Teresa.

"I'm over here," Lui yelled.

"My name is Gary," he said shyly.

"Beth won the race!" they cheered.

"I can't go to the movies," Mark answered sadly.

"We are so high off the ground," Peggy squeaked.

"Where are you?" the child cried.

"Ana broke my bike," Rick stormed.

"What good news!" Juan said excitedly.

"I think I hurt my ankle," moaned Raj.

"I can help you," Hans answered bravely.

"Do you think it will work?" Fran asked thoughtfully.

"What beautiful flowers you have," the clerk said cheerfully.

Published by Frank Schaffer Publications.
Copyright protected.

0-7682-3415-8
101 Easy Reading Games

Silly Stories

 **Silly Story Parts of Speech**

Objective: identify and practice using parts of speech

Materials: Silly Story (page 91), chart paper, marker, tape

Players: partners

Setting: chart paper

Getting Ready: Duplicate the Silly Story. Tape pieces of chart paper on the wall around the classroom. Each pair of students will need one.

How to Play:
1. Have partners number 1 through 20 on chart paper.
2. Call out the numbers from the story and the corresponding part of speech and descriptor.
3. Students write a word to match.
4. Pass out the Silly Story pages and allow students to write their responses.

Published by Frank Schaffer Publications.
Copyright protected.

0-7682-3415-8
101 Easy Reading Games

Name _____ Date _____

An Interesting Find

One day I decided to go visit a _____, who lives in _____.
                                          1. person noun   2. place noun

Since it was _____ mile(s) from my house, I decided I would ride my
                         3. number adjective

_____. I _____ out the door and jumped
       4. thing noun   5. verb

_____ my _____. I was on my way!
      6. preposition   7. thing noun from 4

Along the way, I saw a _____. It had a _____
                     8. thing noun   9. size adjective

_____ and a _____ _____. It was the
     10. thing noun   11. color   12. thing noun

_____ thing I had ever seen! Just looking at it made me want to
   13. adjective with -est

_____. "_____, no one will believe this!" I thought.
     14. verb   15. interjection

I immediately turned around and headed to _____. Someone could help me
                               16. place noun

_____ and put it in a _____. Then I could go on television
     17. place noun   18. thing noun

and tell everyone about my discovery. I would be _____. Every one would want
                                     19. adjective

my _____.
    20. thing noun

0-7682-3415-8
101 Easy Reading Games

Silly Stories

 **Speaking About Silly Stories**

Objective: read interjections and end marks with correct intonation

Materials: completed Silly Story (page 91)

Players: individuals

Setting: classroom

Getting Ready: none

How to Play:

1. Allow volunteers to read their Silly Stories out loud. Encourage them to read interjections and sentences fluently.
2. Ask questions that compare and contrast the stories.
   - Which was the funniest?
   - What words made it funny?
   - What pictures did you see in your mind?
   - What would you like to hear more about?

Silly Stories

 **Cooking Up Some Silly Story Fun**

Objective: understand steps in a process

Materials: Silly Story recipe (page 94), chalk, pencil

Players: individuals

Setting: classroom

Getting Ready: Duplicate the Silly Story recipe for each student.

How to Play:
1. Have students number 1 through 19 on paper.
2. Call out the numbers from the story and the corresponding part of speech and descriptor. Students write a word to match.
3. Pass out the Silly Story pages and allow students to review their stories.

 Comma-cal Recipes

Objective: practice reading commas for fluency

Materials: completed Silly Story recipes (page 94), pencil

Players: partners

Setting: classroom

Getting Ready: none

How to Play:
1. Allow partners to practice reading their Silly Story recipe. They might alternate reading the ingredients and steps. Or one student could read the ingredient list, while the other reads the steps.
2. Invite each pair to read the rhyme for the class.
3. Ask classmates to make positive responses to tell what they liked about each presentation.

Published by Frank Schaffer Publications.
Copyright protected.

0-7682-3415-8
101 Easy Reading Games

Name _____ Date _____

Casserole Surprise Recipe

First, get out _____, _____, and _____.
                    1. a food   2. a food   3. liquid

Second, _____ _____ a _____. Now, put all
             4. action   5. preposition   6. food

of the ingredients into a _____. Then , add _____ teaspoons
                          7. container   8. number

of _____. Next, _____ all the ingredients together with a
    9. seasoning name   10. action

_____. Finally, pour the mix into a _____ pan.
    11. tool   12. size word

Now it is time to cook the casserole. First, put the pan into a _____ to cook for
                                  13. furniture

_____ minutes. When it begins to smell _____, take it out
   14. number   15. adjective

_____. It should have a _____ _____.
 16. adverb with –ly   17. adjective   18. color

Finally, it is time to eat the casserole. Doesn't it taste _____?
                                          19. adjective

Published by Frank Schaffer Publications.
Copyright protected.

0-7682-3415-8
101 Easy Reading Games

 ## Silly Story Song

Objective: identify syllables and rhyming words

Materials: Silly Story song innovation (page 96), paper, pencil

Players: partners

Setting: classroom

Getting Ready: Duplicate the song for partners.

How to Play:
1. Have students number 1 through 14 on paper.
2. Call out the numbers from the story and the corresponding descriptor. Students write a word to match.
3. Pass out the Silly Story pages and allow partners to review their song innovation.

 ## Silly Story Sing-Along

Objective: practice singing rhythmically and at an appropriate rate to develop fluency

Materials: completed Silly Story song innovation (page 96)

Players: partners

Setting: classroom

Getting Ready: Duplicate the song for partners.

How to Play:
1. Allow partners to practice singing their Silly Story song. Encourage them to try different rhythms and rates to find one that matches the mood of the song.
2. Invite each pair to sing the song for the class.
3. Ask classmates to discuss how the rhythm and rate of each innovation affect the mood of the song.

Name _____ Date _____

Silly Story Song Innovation

(Sung to the tune of "Twinkle, Twinkle Little Star.")

_____, _____ _____
  1. two syllable verb   2. repeat 1   3. two syllable adjective

_____.
  4. one syllable noun

How I wonder why you _____?
           5. one syllable verb that
           rhymes with number 4

Up above the _____ so _____
        6. one syllable noun   7. one syllable adjective

Like a _____ in the _____.
      8. two syllable noun   9. one syllable noun that
                rhymes with number 7

_____, _____ _____
  10. repeat 1   11. repeat 1   12. repeat 3

_____,
  13. repeat 4

How I wonder why you _____?
          14. repeat 5

Published by Frank Schaffer Publications.
Copyright protected.
0-7682-3415-8
101 Easy Reading Games

Brain Games

74 Homograph Race

Objective: recognize and practice using homographs

Materials: chalk

Players: teams

Setting: at the board

Getting Ready: Write pairs of sentences using homographs. The sentences should use the words in different ways. Some examples are given below.

How to Play:

1. Divide the class into three teams.
2. Invite the first player from each team to go to the board. Read two sentences out loud.
3. The students write a word that completes both sentences. The first student to correctly name the word gets two points for the team. Players from the other teams get one point if they answer correctly.
4. The team with the most points wins.

Homograph Sentences

park

Mrs. Dante runs in the _____ every day.

Randy wanted to _____ the car in the garage.

fly

Get that black _____ off the food.

Andy has a model airplane that he can _____ with a remote.

bat

A _____ flew out from under the bridge.

After two outs, it was John's turn to _____.

watch

Beto looked at his _____ to see the time.

We sat down to _____ television.

play

Patty is an actress in the _____.

The children went outside to _____ in the snow.

land

Grandma's airplane was going to _____ at the airport soon.

The _____ was being donated to make an animal refuge.

yard

Wes mowed the grass in his _____.

Tia bought a _____ of ribbon to make a pillow.

Brain Games

75 Animal Sound Off

Objective: recognize and practice using onomatopoeia

Materials: none

Players: individuals

Setting: lining up

Getting Ready: none

How to Play:

1. Say an animal's name, followed by a student's name.
2. The student says an onomatopoeia sound word before lining up. Some animals may make several sounds. If you repeat an animal's name, tell students they may not repeat words.

Animal Sound Word Examples

mouse—squeak

cat—meow, purr, hiss

dog—bark, yip, woof

horse—neigh

pig—oink, grunt

bird—chirp, tweet, caw

chicken—cluck

frog—croak, ribbit

cow—moo

snake—hiss

lion—roar

bear—growl

Published by Frank Schaffer Publications.
Copyright protected.

0-7682-3415-8
101 Easy Reading Games

Brain Games

76 Simple as a Simile

Objective: recognize and practice using similes

Materials: none

Players: individuals

Setting: waiting in line

Getting Ready: none

How to Play:

1. Say a student's name followed by a phrase that can be made into a simile.
2. Allow the student about three seconds to answer. If the student does not answer or answers with a response that does not make sense, clap your hands and call on another student to complete the simile.

Simile Starter Examples

Quiet as a	Hairy as a
Smiled like a	Fast as a
Busy as a	Slept like a
Loud as a	Soft as a
Tight as a	Sharp as a
Hard as a	Fought like a
Eager as a	Scared as a
Thick as a	Sour as a
Tiny like a	Sparkled like a
Long like a	Scared as a

Published by Frank Schaffer Publications.
Copyright protected.

0-7682-3415-8
101 Easy Reading Games

Brain Games

 **Shopping Memory**

Objective: practice classifying skills

Materials: none

Players: whole class

Setting: waiting in line

Getting Ready: none

How to Play:

1. Choose a specific kind of store, such as clothes, hardware, or furniture. Begin a sentence starter that names the store from which items can be purchased. For example, "I went to the clothes store to buy some...."
2. The first person in line repeats the starter and names something that can be purchased in the store.
3. Play continues as different students add an item to the starter while repeating the correct order of the words.
4. When two students in a row cannot think of an item, introduce a category and sentence starter.

Story Starters

I went to the furniture store...

I went to the tool store...

I went to the bookstore...

I went to the music store...

I went to the florist...

I went to the sporting goods store...

I went to the craft store...

I went to the computer store...

I went to the appliance store...

I went to a food court...

Published by Frank Schaffer Publications.
Copyright protected.

0-7682-3415-8
101 Easy Reading Games

Brain Games

78 Field Trip Scavenger Hunt

Objective: identify main idea and details

Materials: paper, pencil

Players: partners

Setting: on a field trip

Getting Ready: Before students leave on the field trip, choose ten items that are important to learn when visiting this place. Write sentences giving hints about the item in cloze sentences. Duplicate the page for students.

How to Play:
1. Pass out the duplicated page.
2. Have students review the sentences while traveling to the field trip site.
3. Challenge partners to find the item that correctly completes each sentence and write the name in the blank.
4. Award a privilege to the pair who first completes the page correctly.

Name _____ Date _____

1. A horse wore a ___harness___ around its neck when it was hitched to a wagon.

2. Clothes were scrubbed on a ___washboard___ to get them clean.

Brain Games

79 Puzzled by Words

Objective: learn words to develop automaticity when reading

Materials: Word Puzzle (page 103), reading selection, pencil

Players: reading buddies

Setting: classroom

Getting Ready: Duplicate the graph paper for each student.

How to Play:

1. Tell reading buddies to take turns reading out loud.
2. Each reading buddy listens for words that the partner cannot read smoothly or does not know. The partner writes the list across the top of graph paper.
3. After students have finished reading the text, each partner writes cloze sentences with the list of words and uses them to make a crossword puzzle on the graph paper.
4. Reading buddies exchange puzzles and complete the puzzles, whisper reading the cloze sentences to practice developing automaticity of the difficult words.
5. When the puzzles are complete, reading buddies check the work by reading the sentences out loud to each other.

Name _____   Date _____

Word Bank

wheelchair

paralyzed

breathe

therapy

talented

① w h e e l c h a i r

Across

1. Christopher Reeve used a _____ to move from place to place.

Down

2. He was a _____ actor who could play many parts.

Published by Frank Schaffer Publications.
Copyright protected.

0-7682-3415-8
101 Easy Reading Games

Word Puzzle

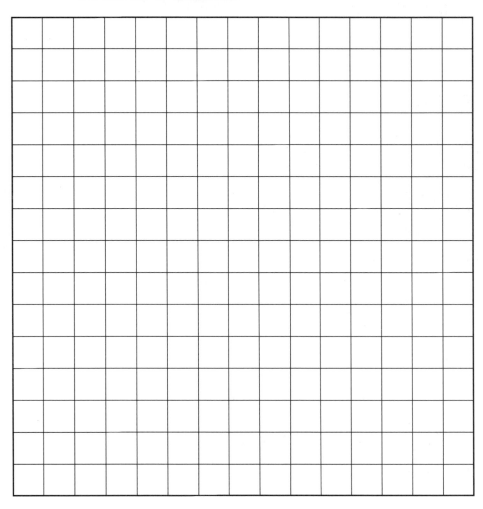

Word Bank

Across

_____

_____

_____

_____

Down

_____

_____

_____

_____

Brain Games

 **Signs of Syllables**

Objective: identify syllables in words

Materials: paper, pencil

Players: individuals

Setting: homework

Getting Ready: none

How to Play:

1. Have students number a paper from 1 through 5 before leaving for the day.
2. Challenge them to look at environmental print (street signs, billboards, store names, package labels, flyers) on the way home and in their house to find at least three examples of words having different numbers of syllables. Encourage them to pay extra attention to words having four and five syllables.
3. Allow students to share their list of words having four or more syllables.
4. For students who complete the assignment, you might allow them to put their papers in a box. Pull out one and award a privilege to the student.

Word Lists

1. stop
2. exit, police, station
3. restaurant
4. categories, accessories, appliances
5. examination, university, organization

Brain Games

81 Compound Scavenger Hunt

Objective: recognize and identify compound words

Materials: newspapers, highlighters, chart paper, tape, marker, clock

Players: small groups of four

Setting: classroom

Getting Ready: Tape sheets of chart paper on the wall of the classroom. Each group will need one.

How to Play:

1. Divide the class into groups of four. Pass out a section of a newspaper to each group.
2. Give students 15 minutes to find and highlight compound words in the text.
3. After 15 minutes, have each group compile the list of their words on chart paper.
4. The group finding the most words wins.

handshakes
rollover
paperwork
spokesman
airport
mailroom

Brain Games

 **Listening for Idioms**

Objective: recognize idioms

Materials: chart paper, markers, tape

Players: small groups of four

Setting: all day

Getting Ready: Tape sheets of chart paper on the wall of the classroom. Each group will need one.

How to Play:
1. Divide the class into groups of four. Assign them one sheet of chart paper.
2. Challenge students to listen for idioms throughout the day.
3. Have them record the idioms on chart paper.
4. At the end of the day, have students read their list out loud.
5. The group with the most idioms should be awarded a treat or privilege.

Extension: Invite students to search the Internet for the origins and meanings of some of the idioms.

Examples

Put your thinking cap on.

I got up on the wrong side of the bed.

She always goes the extra mile.

You are what you eat.

I wash my hands of it.

Knock on wood.

Brain Games

83 Word Wise

Objective: develop an understanding of words

Materials: Word Wise graphic organizer (page 108), pencil, clock

Players: individuals

Setting: after reading a text

Getting Ready: Duplicate the graphic organizer for each student.

How to Play:
1. Choose a word from a text that students should examine for meaning and structure.
2. Write the word on the board.
3. Review the categories on the graphic organizer.
4. Allow students five minutes to complete the graphic organizer.
5. Review the responses and have students calculate their points. They get one point for each correct answer.

Published by Frank Schaffer Publications.
Copyright protected.

0-7682-3415-8
101 Easy Reading Games

Name _____ Date _____

Word Wise Graphic Organizer

Word _____

Definition

Rhyming Words

Family Structure Words

Related Category Words

Synonyms

Sentence

Points _____ (1 point for each item listed)

Published by Frank Schaffer Publications.
Copyright protected.

0-7682-3415-8
101 Easy Reading Games

Brain Games

 **Joking Around with Homographs**

Objective: recognize and practice using homographs

Materials: chart paper, marker, paper, pencil

Players: individuals

Setting: free time

Getting Ready: Write the jokes included here on chart paper.

How to Play:
1. Invite students to solve the jokes.
2. Challenge students to write at least three homograph jokes.
3. Allow students to share the jokes with the class.

Homograph Jokes

Why did the Cyclops close his school?
(He only had one pupil.)

What kind of dog keeps time the best?
(a watch dog)

How do you know that the ocean is friendly?
(It waves.)

Why did the girl go to the cosmetic store after school?
(Her teacher asked her to take a make-up test.)

Why did the man paint a jacket on the house?
(It needed a new coat of paint.)

Published by Frank Schaffer Publications.
Copyright protected.

0-7682-3415-8
101 Easy Reading Games

Brain Games

85 Homophone Poems

Objective: recognize and practice using homophones

Materials: The Walk poem (page 111), paper, pencil

Players: individuals

Setting: classroom

Getting Ready: Duplicate the poem for each student.

How to Play:
1. Challenge students to underline each homophone as quickly as they can.
2. As students finish the work, make sure they have found all the errors. Use the key included here.
3. Challenge students to write a short homophone poem of their own.
4. Allow students to share the poems with the class.

The Walk

The **son** was **hi** up **inn** the sky.
A gentle wind **blue**, **two**.
A little boy went **four** a walk,
Too look **fore sum** thing **too due**.

He said good **buy too** his **ant**,
And headed **two** the **would**.
He took the **rode two** the **write**,
And walked as long as he could.

Along the **weigh** he could **sea**
Awl kinds of interesting creatures.
Their was a **hair**, a **pear** of **dear**,
And a moose with **grate** big features.

The **site** that gave his **hart** a scare,
And **maid** it skip a **beet**
Was a **bare** with **ruff** black **fir**,
And **clause** upon its **feat**.

"**Eye knead too** go," the **buoy** did say,
Sew he quickly ran a **weigh**.
He did **knot chews too meat** that **bare**,
Ore become **it's pray**.

86 Choral Reading

Objective: practice choral reading for fluency

Materials: The Walk poem (page 111)

Players: partners

Setting: classroom

Getting Ready: none

How to Play:
1. Allow partners to practice chorally reading poem. Encourage them to read together with a rhythm.
2. Invite each pair to read the poem for the class.
3. Ask classmates to make positive responses to tell what they liked about each presentation.

Published by Frank Schaffer Publications.
Copyright protected.

0-7682-3415-8
101 Easy Reading Games

The Walk

The son was hi up inn the sky.

A gentle wind blue, two.

A little boy went four a walk,

Too look fore sum thing too due.

He said good buy too his ant,

And headed two the would.

He took the rode two the write,

And walked as long as he could.

Along the weigh he could sea

Awl kinds of interesting creatures.

Their was a hair, a pear of dear,

And a moose with grate big features.

The site that gave his hart a scare,

And maid it skip a beet

Was a bare with ruff black fir,

And clause upon its feat.

"Eye knead too go," the buoy did say,

Sew he quickly ran a weigh.

He did knot chews too meat that bare,

Ore become it's pray.

Brain Games

87 Web Crawler

Objective: identify prior knowledge

Materials: mural paper, markers

Players: small groups of four

Setting: before reading a selection

Getting Ready: none

How to Play:

1. Identify the topic in a story or article.
2. Divide the class into groups of four.
3. Give each group a large sheet of mural paper. Have them spread out on the floor.
4. Tell students to draw a small web that has a center circle and four outer circles in the center of the paper.

5. Identify the topic and have students write the word or phrase in the center circle.
6. Tell students to list four related concepts in the outer circles.
7. Students continue to add circles and related ideas to the web to make a huge concept web.
8. Allow students 15 to 20 minutes to work on the web. Encourage students to include anything that comes to their mind that is related to the topic.
9. Have students walk around to see how the topic expanded in other groups.

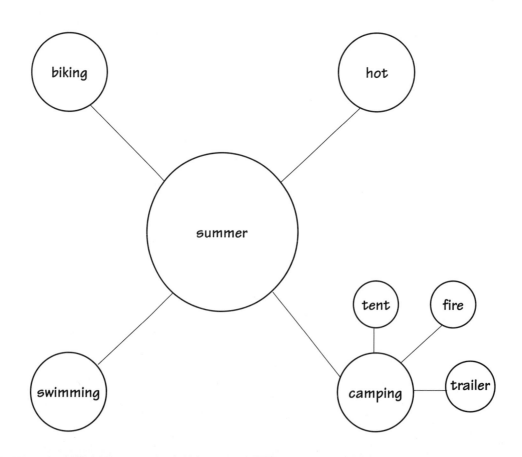

Brain Games

88 Round Robin Stories

Objective: identify story elements

Materials: paper, pencil

Players: whole class

Setting: classroom

Getting Ready: none

How to Play:

1. Have students sit on the floor in a circle.
2. Tell students to write their name on a sheet of paper. Explain they will work cooperatively to write a round robin story.
3. Tell students to write a sentence that tells about a character, including the name.
4. Have students pass the paper to their right. Ask them to read the sentence on the paper.
5. Have students write a sentence that tells about a setting.
6. Have students pass the paper to the right again and read the sentences.
7. Tell them to write a sentence that tells about a problem the character has.
8. Have students continue to pass the paper to the right on your signal. Each time, have them write sentences that create a plot.
9. Finally, have students write a solution.
10. Ask students to find the paper with their name and allow them to read the story.

Published by Frank Schaffer Publications.
Copyright protected.

0-7682-3415-8
101 Easy Reading Games

Brain Games

89 Questioning Characters

Objective: generate questions and answers

Materials: paper, pencil

Players: reading club

Setting: classroom

Getting Ready: none

How to Play:

1. Have each student choose a character from a story that club members have read.
2. Invite a volunteer to the front of the room. Ask the student to imagine he is the character. Tell them to answer in first person.
3. Have the other students take turns asking 20 questions that help identify which character the volunteer chose.
4. Have the volunteer use tally marks to track the number of questions.
5. The first student to identify the mystery character gets to go next. If the character is not guessed, the volunteer selects the next person.

Published by Frank Schaffer Publications.
Copyright protected.

0-7682-3415-8
101 Easy Reading Games

Moving Games

 **Playground Inferences**

Objective: make inferences

Materials: none

Players: individuals

Setting: recess area

Getting Ready: none

How to Play:

1. Have students gather to one side of the recess area.
2. Invite each student to look around and choose a person or group of people.
3. Invite volunteers to point out the group they are looking at and make an inference about the situation. For example, a student might point out that two girls are laughing together. An inference could be that the topic is funny.
4. Encourage them to explain how they made the inference.
5. Invite the remaining students to determine if other inferences could be made concerning the same group.
6. Allow each student to make an inference.

Moving Games

 **Fixin' to Play Baseball**

Objective: understand and practice using prefixes

Materials: none

Players: two teams

Setting: classroom

Getting Ready: Identify four places in the room that will be the bases of the diamond.

How to Play:
1. Divide the class into two teams.
2. Say a word with a prefix. The first player on team 1 stands and spells the word to move to first base. He must identify the prefix to get to second base and the root to get to third base. The player must use the word in a sentence to hit a homerun. The player can say "stop" before moving to the next base to stay on a base. Any incorrect answer gives the team an out.
3. Each time a player makes it home, the team scores a point. A team can "bat" until getting three outs.
4. Team 2 comes up to bat after three outs.
5. Play continues until one team gets 10 runs or time is up.

Words with Prefixes Examples

unorganized	incomplete
unavailable	imperfect
unorganized	impolite
unavailable	impractical
unexpected	submarine
unaware	submerge
unconcerned	subzero
reappear	irresponsible
refresh	irregular
recycle	irregular
reproduce	irrelevant
misfortune	embark
mispronounce	emboss
misunderstand	embrace
injustice	empower

Moving Games

92 Dictionary Basketball

Objective: practice using dictionary skills

Materials: empty trashcan, small ball, tape, transparency, overhead projector, paper strips

Players: teams

Setting: classroom

Getting Ready: Choose words from a dictionary and write the respellings of the words in two columns on a transparency. Place tape on the floor to mark a throwing line.

How to Play:

1. Divide the class into two teams. Team players stand in line behind the throwing line.
2. Place the transparency on the overhead. Cover each column with a strip of paper.
3. Uncover the first word in the first column.
4. The first player on team 1 says the word. If she is correct, she gets a chance to shoot the ball. If she is incorrect, she moves to the back of the line and the first player from team 2 takes a turn to identify the word. The player scores two points if the ball goes in the basket.
5. Play continues with players on each team taking turns identifying the words on the transparency.
6. When the time is up, the team with the most points wins.

Phonetic Respellings

interval (in´ tər vəl)

nomad (nō´ mad)

vast (vast)

priority (prī ȯr´ ə tē)

monument (mon´ yə mənt)

legend (le´ jənd)

avid (a´ vəd)

profile (prō´ fīl)

conductor (kon duk´ tər)

appreciate (ə prē´ shē āt´)

symphony (sim´ fō nē)

peculiar (pi kyo͞ol´ yər)

inquire (in kwī ər´)

dreadful (dred´ fool)

autographs (ô´ tə grafs)

dismay (dis mā´)

admire (ad mīr´)

complicate (kom´ pli kāt´)

demand (di mand´)

creative (krē ā´ tiv)

fantastic (fan tas tik´)

Moving Games

93 Antonym Volleyball

Objective: identify antonyms

Materials: volleyball

Players: two teams

Setting: gym or playground where there is a volleyball net

Getting Ready: none

How to Play:

1. Divide the class into two teams. Six players from each team stand on either side of the court. The rest of the team sits behind their players off the court.
2. The player from Team 1 tosses the ball over and says a word that has an antonym.
3. A player from Team 2 catches the ball and says the antonym. If the word is correct, Team 2 scores a point. That player repeats the process of saying another word that has an antonym and tossing the ball. If the player is incorrect, drops the ball, or repeats a word, a reserve teammate rotates in to take her place on the court.
4. The first team to score 15 points wins the game.

Note: Rotate team members into the game if need be to make sure all students get time on the court.

Moving Games

 **Parts of Speech Four Square**

Objective: recognize and identify parts of speech

Materials: chalk, rubber playground balls, index cards, markers

Players: small groups

Setting: recess

Getting Ready: Make several sets of cards that name the different parts of speech (noun, verb, interjection, adjective, adverb, preposition, conjunction). Draw several four-square courts outside.

How to Play:

1. Divide the class into groups equal to the number of boards. Give each group a set of cards and a ball. Ask each group to go to a four-square court.

2. Four students take their places on the court.

3. The first person waiting in line draws a card without looking and identifies the part of speech. He reshuffles the card in the set.

4. The four players play the game according to the rules but must name an example of the part of speech when the ball bounces in their court. If the ball is missed, a word is repeated, or if the person does not name a word in a timely manner, the player is out.

5. The first person in line rotates in.

6. The process is repeated until time is up.

Moving Games

95 Alpha Toss

Objective: practice dictionary skills by alphabetizing words

Materials: mural paper, beanbags, yardstick

Players: partners

Setting: activity center

Getting Ready: Cut a four-foot length of mural paper. Draw a 4 x 4-unit grid that fills the paper. Write a word from below in each square in any order.

How to Play:

1. Player 1 tosses a beanbag into the square to show the first word in an alphabetical listing of the words. If the beanbag lands in the correct square, the player continues until he misses or the order is incorrect. On his next turn, the player continues with the word he stopped on.
2. Player 2 repeats the process.
3. The game continues until one player has gotten the beanbag in each square to show the alphabetical order of all 16 words.

Words

flag	flail	flair	flake
flame	flamingo	flank	flannel
flap	flare	flash	flat
flattery	flaunt	flavor	flaw

Published by Frank Schaffer Publications.
Copyright protected.

0-7682-3415-8
101 Easy Reading Games

Moving Games

96 1, 2, 3, Go!

Objective: practice fluent reading

Materials: sentence strips, marker, scissors

Players: whole class

Setting: classroom

Getting Ready: Write the sentence parts below on separate sentence strips.

How to Play:

1. Pass out a strip to each student. Have all the students holding subjects form a line. Have all the students with verb strips form a second line. Have all the students with prepositions form a third line.

2. Have the first person in each group step to the front, turn around, and show their cards to the class.
3. All the students need to say the sentence together several times until they can say the words smoothly and fluently.
4. The three students move to the end of the line.
5. Continue the process so that each student gets to lead the class.

Subject	Verb	Prepositional Phrase
The little cat	sat	on the pillow.
The big lion	ran	over the hill.
The funny monkey	swam	in the ocean.
The green monster	lived	under the bed.
The small baby	giggled	under the table.
The pretty flower	smelled	in the vase.
The shiny bike	fell	on the ground.
The loud car	stopped	along the road.
The silver robot	danced	to the music.
The hungry dog	ate	below the bridge.

The cat   smelled   in the vase.

Published by Frank Schaffer Publications.

0-7682-3415-8
101 Easy Reading Games

Moving Games

 Steps in a Process Speed Ball

Objective: identify steps in a process

Materials: tennis ball

Players: whole class

Setting: classroom

Getting Ready: none

How to Play:
1. Have students stand.
2. Name a process.
3. Give one student the ball. She quickly says the first step in the process named and tosses the ball to another student. If that student drops the ball, skips an important step, or cannot quickly say a step, the person sits down and is out of the game.
4. Tell students to toss the ball quickly but carefully. If all the steps are named before the last student is standing, name a new process.
5. The last student standing wins the game. That student names a new process to begin a new game.

Moving Games

98 Tossing the Facts

Objective: recognize facts and opinions

Materials: small balls, large plastic cups

Players: partners

Setting: in the gym, after reading a nonfiction chapter in a textbook

Getting Ready: none

How to Play:

1. Give a ball to partners and a cup to each student.
2. Have partners stand facing each other about a yard apart.
3. Player 1 puts the ball in her cup. She tosses it to her partner.
4. Player 2 catches the ball in her cup and states a fact learned from the text. If Player 2 drops the ball, she states an opinion about the topic.
5. Player 2 tosses the ball back to Player 1, who states a different fact.
6. Both students take a step backwards.
7. Partners repeat the process to continue the game.
8. When both players have dropped the ball, they return to the original position and begin the game again.

Moving Games

 **Compare Relay**

Objective: recognize how things are alike and different

Materials: two boxes, one each of different small toys and tools, such as a paper clip, pencil, toy car, block, counter (enough for each student, plus five more)

Players: teams

Setting: outside during recess or in the gym

Getting Ready: Choose five of the items and hide them in one of the boxes. Place the other items, one for each student, in the other box. Mark a starting point for a relay race. Place the box with the most items at the turning point.

How to Play:
1. Divide the class into two teams. Have them line up at the starting point. Sit between the teams with the box by your feet.
2. On a signal from you, the first runner on each team runs to the box at the turning point and pulls out any item.
3. As the students run, pull out one item from the box by your feet.
4. When the students return, each must tell how the item they have is the same as the item you are holding.
5. If you agree, take the item from the player and put it in your box.
6. When you take the item, the next runner on the team goes.
7. The first team to have each runner complete the course wins.

Moving Games

100 Conclusive Charades

Objective: practice drawing conclusions

Materials: index cards, marker, clock

Players: individuals

Setting: classroom

Getting Ready: Write the action below on index cards. Each student will need one, so include more if needed.

How to Play:
1. Have students choose a card without looking.
2. Tell students to act out the movement for others to guess.
3. The first student to correctly identify the action goes next.

Actions

baking a cake

washing dishes

grocery shopping

fueling a car

building a fire

roller skating

painting a picture

planting seeds

mowing the lawn

making a bed

walking a dog

opening an umbrella

making a sandwich

running a race

playing baseball

rowing a boat

fishing

flying an airplane

playing checkers

building a sand castle

Published by Frank Schaffer Publications.
Copyright protected.

0-7682-3415-8
101 Easy Reading Games

Moving Games

 **Classified Chains**

Objective: practice classifying

Materials: five items in four different categories, such as a hammer, screwdriver, pliers, wrench, and level to make a tool category; four bags; marker

Players: teams

Setting: in the gym

Getting Ready: Spread the items out all over the floor so that items in the same category are not near each other. Write the name of a category on each bag.

How to Play:
1. Divide the class into four equal groups. If the teams are uneven, allow some students to position themselves around the gym to be judges.
2. Have each team line up and form a human chain by holding onto the student's shoulder in front of them.
3. Give the last student in each group a bag and identify the category. Tell the teams they must find the five items that belong in their category.
4. On a signal from you, the teams move around the floor, gathering the items that belong to their category. The lead person picks up the item when he finds it. He passes it to the person behind him.

5. Without breaking the chain, each player passes it behind to the next student. The tail person must get the item in the bag. Only the lead person may pick up an item from the floor, so if something drops, the lead player must move around to get it. If the team breaks the chain, a judge can stop the team. The team members count off before they can move again.

Note: Make sure the items are large enough that the teams can easily see them as they move around.

Sample Categories

<u>Dishes:</u> pan, plate, cup, bowl, mug (all unbreakable)

<u>Toys:</u> doll, block, ball, car, truck

<u>School tools:</u> ruler, stapler, backpack, box of markers, notebook

<u>Clothes:</u> jacket, shoe, hat, sweatshirt, glove

<u>Reading materials:</u> dictionary, textbook, paperback, magazine, newspaper

You might also consider choosing categories with specific characteristics, such as things that are blue, round, soft, or made of plastic.

Published by Frank Schaffer Publications.
Copyright protected.

0-7682-3415-8
101 Easy Reading Games

Skill Index

(Listed by game number.)

Published by Frank Schaffer Publications.
Copyright protected.

0-7682-3415-8
101 Easy Reading Games

Player Index

(Listed by game number.)

Environment Index

(Listed by game number.)

Published by Frank Schaffer Publications.　　　　　　　　　　　　　　　　0-7682-3415-8
101 Easy Reading Games